CLIMBING
MOUNT KILIMANJARO

CLIMBING

MOUNT

KILIMANJARO

Stephen Carmichael
Susan Stoddard

with a new foreword by Rick Ridgeway
and forewords by Neville Shulman
and Robert M. Moore, Jr.

Library of Congress Cataloging-in-Publication Data

Carmichael, Stephen.
    Climbing Mount Kilimanjaro, second edition / Stephen
Carmichael , Susan Stoddard ; with a new foreword by Rick
Ridgeway and forewords by Neville Shulman and Robert M.
Moore, Jr.
        p. cm.
Includes bibliographical references (p.) and index.
   ISBN 0-936741-16-3
   1. Mountaineering--Tanzania--Kilimanjaro, Mount--
Guidebooks. 2. Kilimanjaro, Mount (Tanzania)-- Guidebooks.
I. Stoddard, Susan, 1948-   II. Title.
   GV199.44 . T342 K545 2002
   796. 52'2'0967826--dc21

                        2002008154

Cover art: an original oil chalk drawing by Belinda Belding,
   Lansing, Michigan

Cover design by Horizon Prepress & Design, Bloomington, Illinois

MEDI-ED PRESS
523 Hunter Boulevard
Lansing, Michigan 48910
Tollfree: 1-800-500-8205
Email: Medi.EdPress@verizon.net
Website: www.Medi-EdPress.com

DISCLAIMER: This book is based on the authors' experiences, but
cannot anticipate every contingency faced by each climber. Nor can
this book substitute for a physician's advice as to the advisability of
attempting a climb. The authors cannot guarantee that climbs will be
successful or accident-free, even if all of their recommendations are
followed.

Dedication

*To the memory
of Sue P. Carmichael
1920–2002*

Contents

Contents

Foreword to the Second Edition

Volcanoes are an elite cadre in the ranks of the world's mountains. Whether extinct, dormant or active, they are all tied directly to the earth's innerworks; it's a connection that makes them seem alive, as though their smoke and lava were breath and blood.

When volcanoes rise singularly and largely above their surroundings, they become the elite of the elite. Here the mind's eye sees Chimborazo, Fujiyama, Rainier. When a singular volcano also rises out of surrounding plains that are arid bushlands, and when it rises to an altitude sufficient to safeguard glacial ice, then the mountain is a singular patriarch, a lord of lords. Here the mind's eye sees Kilimanjaro.

Scientists estimate it has been several millennia since Kilimanjaro's last eruption. In geological classification the mountain is dormant. This moniker "dormant" does nothing, however, to diminish Kilimanjaro's grandeur. And its snows, shimmering above the plains studded with umbrella acacias and desert thorn, seem so incongruous they look mythical. When John Rebmann, the German missionary who in 1848 became the first European to see Kilimanjaro, sent home a report stating that he thought the white he saw on top the mountain was snow and ice, his countrymen dismissed him as delusional.

Part of the reason Rebmann was convinced there was snow on top of Kilimanjaro was that the surrounding Wachagga peoples called the white features near the summit "baridi," the same word they used for "cold." This confirmed Rebmann's suspicions, and it also adds to the plausibility that some daring tribesmen had scaled the mountain, or at least ventured high enough to touch the ice and snow, to know firsthand that it was cold. To me, it is also plausible that at least someone of these early tribesmen was lured to the heights for the same reasons that draw modern mountaineers.

I find it impossible to resist gazing up at such a great peak, rising singularly out of arid bushlands, without also wanting to experience the reverse view: to know how those bushlands look when gazing down at them from nearly 20,000 feet above. As the French philosopher and climber René Daumal wrote, "So why do we bother (to climb)? Just this: what is above knows what is below, but what is below does not know what is above."

Climbing Mount Kilimanjaro is a good guide for all those who desire the reverse view, who want to stand at dawn on the rim of the summit caldera and watch the sun rise above those bushlands, backlighting the craggy lava summit of neighboring Mawenzi, glinting yellow off the spectral ice.

Rick Ridgeway

Rick Ridgeway is the author of *The Shadow of Kilimanjaro: On Foot Across East Africa.* He summitted Mount Kilimanjaro on 16 September 1996.

Foreword I to the First Edition

Kilimanjaro is one of the great mountains of the world. It doesn't reach to the extraordinary great heights of Everest and K2 and many other Himalayan mountains but it is the highest in the continent of Africa and anyone who reaches its summit has achieved no mean feat. It is a glorious and beautiful mountain, worthy of any climber's full attention and stands alone in vast open plains, rising majestically to 19,340 feet. You can attempt to climb it by the Tourist Route or by one of the harder routes, in a few days, or more leisurely at a slower pace, but if you manage to stand on the roof of Africa you will experience the kind of exhilaration which comes but rarely in an individual's lifetime.

Kilimanjaro used to be in Kenya but was given to her cousin Kaiser Wilhelm by Queen Victoria as a birthday present and so ended up in Tanzania (previously Tanganyika). It's not everyone who can move mountains!

Climbing Mount Kilimanjaro is an intriguing and stimulating book and deserves its publication. It contains valuable information which cannot be found in other mountain books and is extremely helpful, important and interesting. Anyone who would like to climb Kilimanjaro or indeed any other African mountain would certainly read this book. It should be carried inside a backpack, knapsack, suitcase or even a jacket pocket and referred to constantly and will save the climber, trekker or even tourist no end of trouble. It will be very useful to those who are just traveling through Africa, although I do hope it will encourage many more to climb Mount Kilimanjaro.

Neville Shulman

Neville Shulman is the author of *Zen in the Art of Climbing Mountains, On Top of Africa,* and *Zen Explorations in Remotest New Guinea.* He summitted Uhuru Peak in December 1991.

Foreword II to the First Edition

Where were Stephen and Susan when I needed them? It was my luckless lot in life to have climbed Mount Kilimanjaro BEFORE Stephen and Susan. My climbing friends and I ignored all pre-climb clues that the adventure might be difficult, and I like to think that our struggles were the real inspiration behind this book — not so much because our group did everything the hard way, but more because we were shining examples of the marketplace need for this excellent book.

If an experience is worth doing—and this one is—it's certainly worth maximizing both the enjoyment of the adventure and the chances of reaching the summit. This book will help you do both.

Robert M. Moore, Jr., J.D.

Robert Moore summitted Uhuru Peak on 24 October 1993.

Memorial to Amran Cohen, M.D.

*Dr. Cohen was a noted surgeon and humanitarian
who was active in the Save a Child's Heart Foundation.
He died on Mount Kilimanjaro in August 2001.*

I had the fortunate privilege to have participated with Dr. Amran Cohen on two of his many humanitarian missions to help children around the world. During my short acquaintanceship with him, I found him to be open, caring, inclusive, and compassionate not only to the children he helped but to the team he led. His spirit of giving was contagious and I know that spirit lives on with his team members. He led a diverse team that functions so well together. His leadership will be missed, but his acts will forever be remembered. I hope his life inspires many to follow in his footsteps. He was an adventurous man who enjoyed the beauty of this earth and delighted in it. His interest in climbing Mount Kilimanjaro demonstrates to us all the importance of preparation and respect for one of nature's many beautiful challenges.

Dan J. Hostetler RN, CCP
Mayo Clinic
30 January 2002

Acknowledgments

Patricia A. Barrier, M.D.
Hartmut Bielefeldt, Ph.D.
Allen St.P. Carmichael
Sue P. Carmichael
Wyatt W. Decker, M.D.
William W. Forgey, M.D.
Charles S. Houston, M.D.
Julie Ann Lickteig, M.S., R.D.
Jay W. McLaren, Ph.D.
Peggy A. Menzel, R.D., L.D.
Byron A. Olney, M.D.
Bessie Rucker
Ray W. Squires, Ph.D.
Jan Stepanek, M.D.
Lee H. Stoddard
Rachel R. Stoddard
Jon A. Van Loon, M.D.
Gordon G. Weller, D.P.M.
Conrad J. Wilkowske, M.D.

A lion and lioness on the Serengeti plains

Preface

Climbing Mount Kilimanjaro is intended for the "average" person who is considering climbing to the top of Africa. If you can presently step outside and run one mile in under four minutes, you don't need our recommendations and tips on physical training; if you consider the few thousand dollars that will be required for airfare alone to be "petty cash," then the information on how much this undertaking will cost is too trivial for your concern; if you have walked the Appalachian Trail from one end to the other, then we can't teach you anything about hiking techniques and the requisite equipment; if you are a physician specializing in altitude sickness and tropical medicine, then we can't offer you any useful new medical information. But if you are like most people, that is, like us, and are lacking in one or more of these areas of expertise, and you still want to climb Mount Kilimanjaro, then this book is for you.

Stephen Carmichael
Susan Stoddard

About the authors

Stephen Carmichael resides in Rochester, Minnesota, with his wife, Susan Stoddard, and son Allen, a high school student. Stephen was graduated from Kenyon College with Honors in Biology. He earned a Ph.D. in Anatomy from Tulane University, and was awarded a Doctorate of Science honoris causa from Kenyon College. He is Professor and Chair of Anatomy and Professor of Orthopedic Surgery at the Mayo Clinic. He is a downhill ski instructor for handicapped children, counsels men who have been arrested for domestic abuse, is a SCUBA diver at the Divemaster rank with a certification in Ice Diving, and is a Diver with the Olmsted County Sheriff's Search and Recovery Dive Team.

Susan Stoddard was graduated from Vassar College where she majored in Biology. She earned her Ph.D. in Zoology from Rutgers University and completed a Postdoctoral Fellowship in Neurosciences at the New Jersey Medical School. She was on

Stephen and Susan above Horombo Huts

Acacia tree over the Serengeti plains

the faculty at Indiana University School of Medicine as a tenured Professor of Neuroscience. She and Stephen Carmichael have collaborated on many scientific investigations, resulting in co-authoring 28 abstracts, 15 articles, and two books. Dr. Stoddard is currently a Technology Licensing Manager at the Mayo Clinic. She is an avid gardener and a SCUBA diver at the Master Diver rank.

1 — A hiker's diary

This is the diary that I (Stephen) kept on Mount Kilimanjaro. It is included here to give you a flavor of what to expect each day when climbing the Marangu Trail. This is verbatim, as I wrote it at the time. Last names and other identifiers have been left out.

[This first-person account of the authors' ascent to the top of Mount Kilimanjaro has been brought from the appendix to become chapter 1 in this second edition; some of the terms and hiking techniques discussed in the narrative may be unfamiliar to some readers, but will be expanded upon in the chapters to follow. —ed.]

27 February 1996, Tuesday

Arrive JRO 9 P.M., fairly easy to clear vaccination record control, passports, baggage claim (bags already there!) and customs. Marangu Hotel has a sign with both our names. Loaded into van and headed to Marangu Hotel. Roads varied <u>widely</u> in

Our first view of Mount Kilimanjaro from the grounds of the Marangu Hotel. Kibo Peak is to the left, Mawenzi is to the right.

quality. Smooth 2-lane road @80 KPH to driving on the shoulder when that was the smoothest. Susan picked out the Southern Cross. Cool! About 1 1/2 hours to Hotel. Led to dining room for cookies and tea. Then 4 porters carried our bags overland to our room. A FAX from my secretary and an email message from the gang in Susan's office lifted our spirits, which weren't exactly sagging. Quick shower (water not very warm) and played cards (Spite & Malice) for a while. Tomorrow begins our climb!

28 February

Did hear some dogs barking during the night, but slept well. Met Seamus Brice-Bennett who seems like an awfully nice chap. Two women came to our room and went through our stuff with us. We are well equipped. Had breakfast of corn flakes and fried eggs. Seamus briefed us for about half an hour. We met our guides, Protas and Isadori, my personal porter, Alphonse, Susan's personal porter, Michael, and 3 other porters with food. Seven of them, two of us. Rather embarrassing! Finally, ready to go. We pile into a truck, make two stops for groceries on the 5 km drive to Marangu Gate. We sign in the log book, and head up the Mountain! It's 12:45 P.M.. The first few hundred meters is paved. Settled into a nice easy pace. It's sunny and hot in spots, shady and cool at other spots. Occasional cool breeze. Stop halfway at a table for lunch. A couple of very cute Norwegian girls on their way down are there. While we're eating, a Toyota Land Cruiser lumbers by. It's a park vehicle with a red cross, suggesting a medical problem above. While we're eating, a dozen or so Colobus monkeys move through the trees overhead. Took photos, of course. Back on the trail, it gets steep and narrow in spots. The Land Cruiser has stopped. Further up we meet an old (> than we) guy who says he's hurt his back. Maybe that was the problem. See a few, not many, people coming down. No one other than our porters going up. Alphonse is with us the whole way.

Horombo Huts. Porters are cooking dinner in the hut in the center of the picture.

The forest changes from cypress to other trees. After 3 hours of walking, we come to a group of A-frame huts. Mandara Hut is the large central hut. We get half a small hut (#8) that luckily is nearest the bathrooms. Finish our first roll of film. Our shirts are soaked with sweat. Change into dry shirts and hang the others up to dry.

Dinner is served, and the portions are enormous. The first course is mushroom soup. Actually tastes pretty good, but looks for all the world like dirty dishwater. Lots of fluid intake. Then a large plate of spaghetti, roasted potatoes, and a cooked vegetable, maybe cabbage. Then some meat that we are told is "cow." Doesn't taste too bad, but our boots would have been easier chewing. More than we could eat. After dinner we played Spite & Malice by the dim light of the big hut while we drank tea. The night sky is fantastic. The gibbous moon is impressive, but the stars put on a sparkling show. Can pick out the Southern Cross and Orion. Sleep like a rock.

29 February, Leap Day

Wake up with the sun, ~6:15. Wash up, after a fashion, and have a big breakfast. Eggs and meat, corn flakes. We've figured out the deal with the daypacks. You carry whatever you will need that day. Our packs are lighter today. More clothes and less heavy stuff. Set off for a long day of hiking ~7:30. Soon we are at the rim of an old crater, Maundi. We circumnavigate the rim, then head up toward Horombo. The scenery changes every 15 minutes. For the most part, we're in high alpine meadow. See a hawk circling overhead, then turns into the wind so he's almost motionless. Then he folds his wings and dives toward the ground. Can't tell if the dive met with success. We get beautiful views of Mawenzi Peak and Kibo Peak. Since Mawenzi is closer, it appears larger. There is a lot of upping and downing, the low points punctuated with a small stream. Muddy and boggy in spots. The clouds come and go below us, affording glimpses of the countryside below. Horombo Hut appears suddenly. It's actually a small village (with room for ~120 people plus guides and porters) of the same style of A-frames as at Mandara. We share a small half-hut with a young Japanese fellow who we think has just been to the top. His English is as extensive as our

Stephen at Zebra Rocks

Giant lobelia with Mawenzi in the background

Japanese. Have some time in the afternoon. Dinner is rice and vegetables and cow. Tomato soup is delicious. This reminds me, along the trail was about 100 yards of rice that had apparently spilled from a container. It somehow struck me as amusing. Wonder what kind of creature(s) will come eat the rice? Susan and I take the two lower side bunks, the Japanese fellow the upper back bunk. We are playing Spite & Malice on the floor when he comes in. He looks vaguely amused. We go to bed.

1 March

This is our "day of rest" at Horombo. Protas suggests that we see The Saddle. This is the same route we will be taking tomorrow. Some of the landmarks are Zebra Rocks and Last Water. Zebra Rocks are rather interesting and lovely. At times water trickles in from above them and leaves light and dark streaks of mineral deposits. We take a photo. Last Water is a damp spot that may have some significance to some people. We hike for a couple of hours and then rather suddenly emerge onto The Saddle. It is a breathtakingly beautiful sight, with Kibo Peak looming up out of the barren, bleak landscape. Susan is moved to tears, and I need to explain to Protas that she is okay. He goes over and puts his arm around Susan to comfort her. It's quite touching. We have lunch and then hike back to Horombo. It's longer going back down than it was coming up. I know that doesn't make sense, but it does seem that way. Our bunkmate tonight is a Canadian named John. He works at finance/banking in Abu Dhabi. He's a very talkative fellow. Tells us that Kibo Hut is cold and damp. We have tomato soup, pasta, veggies, and meat. We play cards for a short while and go to bed.

2 March

Awake bright and early and have breakfast by 6:30. Porridge. We take the Upper Route out of Horombo toward Mawenzi, the same route as yesterday. Pass Zebra Rocks and Last Water. The day is beautiful, again. We have met a couple from Indiana. He's a Baptist minister and she works at the church. They are a few years older than we. They pass us. Also, a group of Austrians pass us, including a ~70 year old lady. Very impressive. The walk along The Saddle is awe-inspiring. Kibo looms larger and larger. We stop at The Rocks, where the Lower Route connects, for lunch. Then it's a moderately difficult hike up to Kibo Hut. The Hut is quite unimpressive. Fortunately, we are put in a room for 12 people with just 4 others, an American family. Richard, a recently-retired dentist, his wife Nadine, who worked in the practice, and their two daughters, one 14, the other 11. The girls are beautiful and exotic. I had heard the 11-year-old pointing out a mouse at Horombo Hut, and I commented that I had been impressed with how calmly she acted. We gave Richard one of our disposable "toothbrushes" for his professional opinion, and he agreed with us, they flunk.

We are fed dinner early and go to bed. We are to arise at midnight. Can't sleep at all. Noise in the hall, people coming into our room looking for other people. There are two Norwegian soldiers who are strong and handsome, and quite sick. Three Alaskan physicians we had met are there. He has a cold, the two women are okay. I find out his name is Shawn (Sean?). When I mention that I teach at Mayo Medical School, he gives me the name of one of my former students! It's a small world.

My student had done a clerkship with him in Alaska. Anyway, a thoroughly dreadful evening is spent not getting any sleep. Susan and I get up to pee a couple of times; what an adventure. Don't ask about the facilities. It's a unisex 3-holer. Modesty has vanished into the thin air, and it sure is thin. At 11:30, Susan and I decide to get up and get dressed. Several layers of our Minnesota finest. Like a couple of Michelin tiremen, we sit down to eat the cookies and tea they bring us at 12:00.

3 March, a day that is burned into my memory

Soon after we finish the cookies and tea, Susan and I set off up the mountain. The moon is nearly full and behind us. We are confident that Protas and Isadori will catch up to us. All too soon we get "Intro to Scree 101." We trudge through this crap, and it gets worse and worse. We're talking about gravel, with rocks ranging from basketball size to dust. Every, single, step, is uncertain. Sure enough, Protas and Isadori catch up, but even they are working hard. After several hours, we reach Hans Mayer Cave. Several people have turned back. The Norwegian soldiers, the male Alaskan MD, many others I don't recognize.

The wind has picked up considerably, the temperature has dropped. The moon is setting over Kibo in front of us and we are on The Snake. The head lamp that my folks gave me proves to be invaluable. I make a mental note to recommend to others that they time the moon a little better. The Snake is pure misery. Back and forth, forth and back. I try to set a slow but steady pace, but it is impossible. Poor Susan keeps sliding back down into me. She is really making things difficult, but she is trying her best. I try to give her words of encouragement. I can't tell if it helps or not. After a few crying jags, she pulls herself together, and she's stronger than ever.

But The Snake stretches on into eternity. This night will never end! It's getting light behind Mawenzi. Slowly but slowly the sun sneaks up on us. I stop and take a photo or 2. We are finally entering The Boulders, which is like climbing over refrigerators with scree in between. I can envision a T-shirt that says

SCREE SUCKS! It really does. The Baptists from Indiana come down. They made it to Gilman's Point. That reintroduces the concept that there is an end in sight.

After the longest time, and now in direct sunlight, Gilman's Point is above us. We reach it, totally out of breath. I feel like collapsing, but I tell myself that I am not passing this way again and if I'm ever going to Uhuru Peak, it will happen today. We can see Uhuru, it's <u>WAY</u> over there and quite a bit above our present position. I am <u>thoroughly</u> intimidated. Susan, bless her soul, suggests that we strike off and see how far we can get. I am able to move out with Isadori at a somewhat brisker pace than Susan and Protas. But brisk would be an exaggeration here. I walk 100 steps, pressure breathing with each and every step, then stop for 100 pressure breaths, counting them off in tens, in ten different languages. Repeat, repeat, repeat.... At certain vantage points I look back and Susan and Protas are still moving toward me. The glaciers seem to be gaining on them, but they are moving forward. I stop and ask Isadori to go back and "help Mama." I stay behind a rock, out of the fierce wind, about 100 meters from Uhuru Peak. I look several times, but they aren't coming yet. I think about how upset Susan's parents will be if Susan dies up here. At the funeral, I will point out to them that they raised a stubborn daughter.

After half an hour, but it seems longer, Susan and our guides appear, and they're close. Protas and Isadori are almost dragging Susan. She collapses dramatically. After a minute or so, she can stand up and we trudge over to the marker at the Top of Africa. Susan asks why I waited for her. I tell her that I knew she'd be coming. I take several photos with the 20 mm (wide angle) lens and with the stereo camera. I can't change lenses because my fingers are too cold. I take out a rock that I'd carried from the bottom and place it at the top for Mark and T. Walley and my other friends who have died. We don't spend too long at the top.

Susan gracefully arriving at Uhuru Peak, flanked by Protas and Isadori

We work our way over to Gilman's Point. We don't see any other hikers, which means we are the last to reach Uhuru today. At Gilman's Point there is an Australian film crew doing a show for The Learning Channel. It will be called "On Top of Africa" or something like that. Susan is so exhausted, and we still have a ways to go. It is hard going down the scree, but nothing compared to coming up it. It's been a very long day already by the time we get to Kibo Hut, and we still have to walk to Horombo! We finally make it to Kibo Hut. Michael greets us with an orange drink and congratulates us. I am very proud. He fixes us a light lunch. And we head out for the 3-hour walk to Horombo. We take the Lower Route, bypassing The Saddle. Each rise seems to promise a view of Horombo but we are repeatedly disappointed. Protas points out some buffalo on the horizon. They're about 1 km away and I can't see them well. We get to Horombo just before sunset. We have been hiking almost continuously for 18 hours! I am too tired to eat. After soup, I crash.

4 March

Protas wakes us at 6:30. I get up from a sound sleep and am surprised that I am not in more pain. Several blisters on my feet are sore, and my ankle aches (a reminder of a sky diving injury), but otherwise I am almost human. We have porridge for breakfast and strike out for Mandara Hut, having lunch there. Seeing the folks sweatingly trudging up past us gets me to wondering who will make it and who won't. Of course, the odds are most won't. We stop for a break at the table and see many black monkeys playing in the trees. The other tourists have not seemed to notice them until we point at them, then the cameras and camcorders come flying out.

Shortly before the Marangu Gate, Protas is met by his 2 daughters, who are quite lovely, and we march on alone. I have the chance to tell Susan how very proud I am of her for making it to the top. I feel like a different person for having accomplished such a difficult feat. We buy T-shirts and lots of post cards at the Gate. The guides, porters, and we pile into the back of the truck for the 5 km ride down to the Hotel. We present tips and gifts to our staff. A Sony Walkman to Protas, $40 to Isadori, $20 to each porter, plus a T-shirt from home to our personal porters, Alphonse and Michael. We also give them lighters, pens, and stickers. We treat them to a couple of beers and they treat us to a song about Kilimanjaro. Good show!

Protas gives us our certificates that look quite official. Susan is #1492 and I'm #1493 for 1996. That's about 25 people per day who make it to the top. We have dinner at the hotel with the folks from Indiana. The real delight is getting cleaned up. I brush my teeth 4 times before the rinse water looks clean. We were really filthy. We make a list of things we did right, and things that we could have improved upon. We decide to write a book about it!

2 — So you want to climb Mount Kilimanjaro!

You must begin with the question: "Why?" This you must first ask yourself, and you must receive a very good answer. You must be satisfied with your answer for several reasons: you will be dedicating yourself for several months to relatively intense physical training; you will spend five or six days under strenuous conditions asking yourself this same question, over and over, and you must accept your answer each and every time; you will be committing considerable financial resources to accomplish your goal.

A second reason you must answer this question is because your friends will ask you again and again. Some will be skeptical, some will be supportive, but they all want to know: "Why?" Satisfying them is not nearly as important as satisfying yourself, but this question will come up, repeatedly.

Okay! Why? There may be as many answers as there are people spread out across Mount Kilimanjaro on any one day. Of the many people we met on the mountain in February/March 1996, several did not have a specific motivation, but rather were in that part of Africa and thought it would be a "cool" thing to do. Of those people, we don't know of any who made it to the top.

The best answer, of course, is up to you. But for many, the answer lies in the realm of a personal challenge. Do you want to challenge yourself physically, as well as mentally, to accomplish something that relatively few people are able to do? Are you successful in your personal and professional life, but want to push yourself a little harder? We think that it is imperative that you develop some reasons along these lines, in addition to other reasons, because the time will come (as when you're in the neighborhood of Gilman's Point) that you will need all of the motivation that you can muster. Gilman's Point marks the edge of the crater rim that is a goal for many climbers of Mount Kilimanjaro.

Whatever your reason, one of the benefits of this undertaking is an increase in your level of physical fitness. Whereas this should not be your only motivation, it will be one of your goals. If you consider yourself to be "athletically challenged" (a politically correct way of admitting to yourself that you are out of shape and/or overweight), then preparation to climb Mount Kilimanjaro will provide you with a focus for the work ahead of you. This will take three to six months (or longer) and if you are to make a sincere attempt to get to the top, you will get yourself into better shape (see chapter 5).

Another motivation is the beauty of the experience. Whereas the living conditions on Mount Kilimanjaro may be a bit more primitive than those to which you are accustomed (and this may be an understatement), the natural beauty is fantastic and a motivation in itself. However, some of the hardest climbing is done at night when the natural beauty won't be available to spur you on! Nevertheless, the experience of climbing up through five distinct climatic zones (from hot equatorial Africa just 3° south of the Equator up to a permanent ice cap) with the scenery changing dramatically two or three times per hour, looking out over the clouds, seeing stars at night that don't appear to twinkle because there is so little atmosphere between you and them, is worth the trip. But this isn't why you're doing this. It's for some reason that is intensely personal and important to you.

So ask yourself: "Why?" And after you are satisfied with the answer, read on.

3 — Can I do this?

Now that you've done the preliminary mental preparation (there is more about that to come later), you need to turn your attention to the physical and the financial. If your health does not permit such a strenuous activity, you need to modify your plans. Find something doable that will present you with a suitable challenge and reward. Getting to Tanzania, up the mountain, and back home will take some time and money (see below, in this chapter). If you don't have enough of either, pick an activity closer to home and probably at a lower altitude.

The first concrete step that you need to take is to get an examination from your physician. You are probably overdue for your physical anyway, so this does not represent an additional expense or bother. Explain to your physician that you intend to climb Mount Kilimanjaro. If he or she doesn't have a firm grasp of the physical and medical consequences of your intentions, please ask him or her to read this book.

It has become almost trite in our society to read instructions such as "consult a physician before undertaking this activity," but we really mean it this time! You will be subjecting your body to considerable stress, and as important as your goal may be, it isn't worth risking your health.

One of the specific medical tests that we would recommend for those over 50 years of age, those who have not been involved in a fitness program for more than one year, or those who have a history of high blood pressure, high cholesterol, obesity, smoking, heart disease, or a strong family history of heart disease, is called a "stress EKG." This test involves taping electrodes to your chest and back, then walking/running on a treadmill (or pedaling a stationary bike) to the point of exhaustion. The performance of your heart is monitored throughout the test. This test most closely simulates what you will asking your body to do on Mount Kilimanjaro. The additional benefit of this test is that it will give you a baseline for your level of physical fitness, and it will be easier for your physician to assist you to get into better shape.

We can't overemphasize that it is absolutely essential that you have your physician's approval before you further consider climbing Mount Kilimanjaro. If your physician recommends that you don't attempt it, listen!

If you enjoy good health and your physician has certified this, continue your preparation. It is likely that there are certain medical conditions that need to be attended to. For example, perhaps your blood pressure is a little too high. With your physician's help, lower it. The kind of advice we're giving here is just common sense and is not related to climbing a mountain. You should be doing this anyway.

After your medical condition has been approved and any concerns addressed, you may next want to look at the financial aspects of this undertaking. It will be expensive. The major expense, by far, will be airfare. We will discuss other considerations in chapter 6, but for now you want to get a rough idea of what it will cost. Call your travel agent and find out how much it is to fly from your home to Amsterdam, The Netherlands, and then from Amsterdam to Kilimanjaro International Airport (JRO). It will be a large number of dollars. Now figure an additional $1,000 per person for the climb. This gives you an idea of the absolute minimum this adventure will take. As we'll discuss later, there will likely be additional costs, but by now you will have an idea whether this trip is affordable.

4 — With whom do I go or go it alone?

Whether to go alone or with a group or a partner is your next question to answer. We did encounter several people on Mount Kilimanjaro who were by themselves. This isn't technically true, because you are required by Tanzanian law to hire a guide, but other than that they were solo. This may suit some people just fine, but we would not be among them.

This is an intense experience that you probably will want to share with at least one soul mate. But this needs to be a person you are very close to. We are an ol' married couple, so this wasn't a hard decision for us, but we joked about the fact that climbing Mount Kilimanjaro would not be a fun first date! You will be living for several days under very primitive conditions where toilet (latrine) facilities are exceedingly basic and a

Susan and Stephen with Mawenzi in the background

bath is out of the question. You will be sleeping together in cramped huts, sometimes with complete strangers (who don't necessarily speak your native language).

It is our recommendation to team up with at least one other person with whom you can train, share expenses, and partake of the experience together. We have heard that this has backfired, with people becoming extremely angry with one another, even breaking off engagements, and it wouldn't surprise us if marriages have been put at risk. Like we said, this is intense.

We also advise that you don't talk somebody into going with you if they are reluctant to undertake this daunting task. This is almost guaranteed to come back to haunt you, most likely at a very inopportune time. This could spoil the whole thing for both (all) of you.

If your spouse is not a possibility, we would suggest that you find at least one other person to climb with you. Ideally, this would not only be a soul mate, but someone with similar athletic ability (or lack thereof), similar financial status (to make sharing of expenses seem fair), and the same love of exotic travel that you have. As you will surmise, your partner has to have the same high level of motivation that you do.

Your other choice is to go it alone. And maybe this suits you well. In any case, it would be preferable to go by yourself than to have an uncooperative partner.

As to some additional considerations to agree on with your partner(s), we have some suggestions. First, the pace is set by the slowest individual, generally the least physically fit. This may sound obvious, but you need to agree to this early on. Second, it must be understood that each person needs to be wholly responsible for him/herself. It's an old rule of mountaineering that people take responsibility for their own success or failure. The decision to continue or not must be each individual's choice, and each is free to continue on without the other(s). When you have a partner who wholeheartedly signs on to that, you're ready for the next phase.

5 — Training, training, and more training

Now your work begins. Depending on your level of physical fitness, and this was determined in your exercise stress test, you have several weeks, or more likely months, of physical training to do. It is our recommendation to allow at least three months to get in as fit a condition as possible. We worked strenuously for seven months, and as we stood on top of Mount Kilimanjaro we did not feel overtrained! It's hard! Jon Krakauer, in his personal account of the Mount Everest disaster that happened just two months after we climbed in Africa, characterized the ascent of 19,340-foot Kilimanjaro as "…physically grueling but technically undemanding…" We would concur. (The book we are referring to is *Into Thin Air*, ©1997 by Jon Krakauer, Villard Books.)

Stephen at Marangu Gate. The signpost lists the places, "suggested" hiking times from place to place, and vegetation zones as you ascend the mountain.

A word about the topography. Mount Kilimanjaro has two peaks, Mawenzi on the east and Kibo to the west. The Marangu Route comes from the east, so Mawenzi looms large at first, although it's about 2,000 feet lower than Kibo. Mawenzi is a volcanic core, presenting sheer cliffs of lava and a very difficult technical climb. Kibo is a volcanic crater, with the west end of the rim being the highest. This is the location of Uhuru Peak.

The Saddle, as is typically used to describe mountain features, is the relatively low, curving part between Mawenzi Peak and Kibo Peak. It's strewn with boulders and other volcanic debris, as well as tiny plants and flowers that are typical of high alpine vegetation, and if you were to take a walk on the moon, it would probably look like this.

We climbed the mountain via the Marangu Trail, which is variously known as the "Tourist Route," the "Coca-Cola Route," or the "Easy Way." And it *is* fairly easy, until that last day! After you have researched the various other routes up Mount Kilimanjaro, you will most likely choose the Marangu Trail (most people do). It begins to the east of the mountain at the Marangu Gate, which is at the village of Marangu in Tanzania. The point here is that even if you go up the "Easy Way," you still need to be in the best physical shape possible.

To give you a better idea of the route, here is a map and our timetable: on day 1 we hiked through lush forest to Mandara and on day 2 through high alpine meadow to Horombo. An extra day at Horombo gave us time to go up the steeper route, past Zebra Rock and Last Water to the eastern edge of The Saddle. On day 4 we repeated our climb to The Saddle and walked west across the high alpine desert to Kibo Hut. Day 5 started at midnight as we left Kibo Hut to ascend via The Snake and over The Boulders to Gilman's Point. Another two hours around the south edge of Kibo crater brought us to Uhuru Peak, the true top of Kilimanjaro. The day finished with the journey down Kibo Peak, past Kibo Hut, and via the Lower Route to Horombo. Day 6 was an easy descent from Horombo to the park entrance.

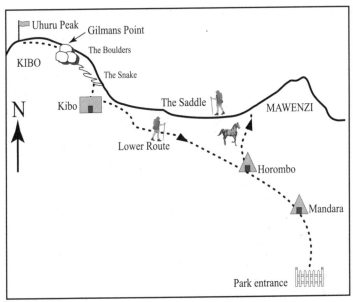

Map of the Marangu Trail route up Mount Kilimanjaro to Uhuru Peak. The trip to the summit took four and a half days; the descent took one and a half days.

The really bad news is that good physical conditioning does not guarantee that you will not develop some form of altitude sickness. However, you can be guaranteed that if you are in poor shape, you won't make it.

Of course, the choice of workout routines is up to you. We concentrated on going up Mount Kilimanjaro, but coming down is a concern as well. The energy requirement for going downhill is about one-third that for going up. It is important to strengthen your quadriceps and other lower limb muscles for the steep descent as well as increasing your cardiopulmonary capacity. Leg presses may help strengthen your legs. Training by walking down steep terrain may not be a good idea, since this will increase your risk for training injury. As we will mention later, using poles on the way down the mountain will decrease your chances of injury and may also decrease muscle soreness.

We emphasized three aspects in our training: aerobic capacity, decreased fat mass (percent body fat), and maintained or increased lean body mass (amount of skeletal muscle). Of course these are interrelated, but all are important. The aerobic capacity is what you will need for endurance, and the fat versus muscle mass is a polite way of pointing out that any extra fat you have on your body is excess baggage that you will have to carry a long way. The more you can trim your body down to a mean, lean climbing machine, the better off you will be. You will need to make your body more efficient to meet the mountain's requirements for endurance, balance, and strength. One of the benefits will be to minimize muscle soreness.

From the data collected during your exercise stress test, your doctor will tell you your maximum heart rate. This number is likely to be close to that calculated by subtracting your age from 220. Using this number, calculate your target heart rate in the range of 65 to 80 percent of maximum; your doctor will suggest the exact percentage. Your goal during your aerobic exercise training will be to maintain this target heart rate for longer and longer periods.

Pick an activity that is as pleasant as possible for you, because you will be doing a lot of it. There are three additional points that are very important: warm up before you get to the strenuous exercise, cool down afterwards, and incorporate a generous amount of stretching into your routine.

In terms of specifics, there are probably as many different exercise routines that are very effective as there are people who want to climb Mount Kilimanjaro. We would recommend a program that mimics the activity of climbing, such as an inclined treadmill or stair-climber. We will offer what we did as examples. But we emphasize, these are only examples; you need to do something that you enjoy (relatively) and that is effective for you. Another example of a "training programme" is offered in appendix A. This is reproduced with permission of Neville Shulman from his book *On Top of Africa, The Climbing of Kilimanjaro and Mt. Kenya.* Unfortunately, the book is now out of print.

Mr. Shulman not only climbed the "Hard Way," but he did it with a severely injured knee. His climb involved raising funds for the National Children's Home in London, and he is clearly an exceptional person. Some of you may find his "training programme" a bit too aggressive and may opt for a longer, more gradually increasing program, which is what we did.

Upon advice from my doctor, I (Stephen) worked out on an inclined treadmill that I set up at home. For any session I could set the incline (it was at maximum within a few weeks). The principal advantage to this arrangement is that a television set could be placed in front of the treadmill, so I had the chance to catch up on a lot of movie videos. After some easy stretches, I climbed onto the treadmill with the TV and VCR remote conveniently placed on a shelf. A fluid source (water) was also within easy reach. A fan was set up to blow vigorously on me, and a towel to mop up the sweat that didn't evaporate was also useful. As for the fluid, you will need a liter or more on hand as your workouts lengthen.

Before starting, I would clip a device on my earlobe that constantly monitored my heart rate. My ultimate goal was to maintain my heart rate at or above 150 beats per minute for two hours. I tried to reach a heart rate of 150 beats per minute within five minutes. This marked the beginning of my workout. At the very beginning I could maintain the 150 beats per minute for about 20 minutes and still be comfortable. I increased this by about five minutes per week, working out as often as possible, but at least five times a week. It wasn't too long before the workout became too long for the time I had available, so a modification was made. Every weekday I would keep my heart rate up for 30 minutes (not counting warm-up or cool-down, which we haven't discussed yet); on weekends I would do it once for at least 60 minutes. I was able to get up to the 120 minutes after three months.

At the end of the predetermined time period I decreased the incline on the treadmill and walked at a comfortable pace for at least five minutes. My heart rate would come down to about 100 beats per minute by this time. Next was stretching, particularly of the lower limb muscles, and most particularly the gastrocnemius and Achilles' tendon (back of the calf). Stretches were held for 30 seconds to a minute. Doing this (warm-up, 30 minutes at 150 beats per minute, cool-down, and stretching) was considered my "minimal" workout. I did this or more almost every day for about seven months.

If time allowed, I added a weight training routine to the end of the workout. This is the part to add that "lean body mass" (muscle). My usual routine was biceps curls, bench presses, military presses, leg presses, and crunches (shortened sit-ups). I worked with weights that allowed me to do three sets of 15 repetitions, being close to maximal effort on the 15th rep. Add on another 100 crunches at the end, followed by stretching, now emphasizing the upper body. I was able to gradually, but steadily, increase the weight for each exercise by doing this about four times a week. My main problem was time, but I felt the aerobic workout was more important, and I still think that is correct. The upper body strength did play an important role when making the final push to the summit using walking sticks. This workout also reduced my percentage of body fat, which would have been just additional "baggage" for me to carry up the mountain.

Susan's training routine was a bit different, but aimed at the same goals. She belongs to a local health club and has had over ten years experience with weight training. For this climb, she worked with a personal trainer twice a week over six months. Her trainer used a classic training schedule, varying exercises each time, but training the muscles of the whole body with 10 to 12 exercises, using primarily free weights, with two sets of 8 to 12 repetitions for upper body and 12 to 15 repetitions for lower body. On the days she did not work with her personal trainer, Susan performed 60 minutes of aerobic exercise, concentrating on an inclined treadmill (up to 25 percent grade) or the escalator-type stairclimber.

Training may also involve loss of weight or body fat, as it did for us. If you are an athlete, then you may wish to adjust your diet for endurance training; this is not what we discuss here. We were just two "average" folks who needed to increase our fitness level and lose fat. There are many popular weight-loss plans, perhaps because everyone is different. The "rules of thumb" are decreasing caloric intake and increasing caloric expenditures through exercise. You may need to experiment to find what works best for you. Keep a food diary. Try different eating patterns, such as eating 4 to 6 smaller meals, rather than the standard 3. Try a vegetarian diet. Over time, we as humans seem to have been most successful in losing weight by eating a more "natural" diet, that is, less processed foods, more fruits and vegetables. Use whatever resources are available to you (a dietitian, a trainer at a local health club, the web) to learn as much as you can, then try different patterns and strategies until you find what works best for your body and lifestyle.

You might wish to try protein shakes (such as Met-Rex), protein supplements (Designer Protein), or skim milk powder to increase your protein consumption without the fat found in many meats. Shop wisely, however, and make sure that the product you choose does not also have a high percentage of calories in carbohydrates.

If you're still with us, and still determined to climb Mount Kilimanjaro, we can let you in on a secret. One of the biggest benefits we realized from this undertaking was a substantial increase in our level of fitness. We were able to take another exercise stress test a few weeks before leaving for Africa, and a 20 percent increase in each of our fitness levels was demonstrable. This was very encouraging! Susan lost weight, I gained weight (lean body mass!). We each decreased our body fat by more than 5 percent and we felt better than we had in years. For many of you, this improvement in your physical fitness will be one of the primary benefits of your decision to climb this mountain.

6 — Making arrangements

In between your workouts, holding down your day job, meeting your responsibilities as a member of a family, and other obligations that you have, it's now time to start planning your trip. When you can go, how long you can stay, and other personal decisions need to be made. Then there are lots of details to attend to: flight reservations, hotel reservations, arrangements in Africa, etc.

When to go

First, there are some seasonal considerations in Africa. In the region of Mount Kilimanjaro there is said to be a "short rainy season" (in October and early November) and a "long rainy season" (from March to June). If at all possible, go during the "dry" seasons. Some people say that January, February, and September are best, with July, August, November, and December also being good.

The full moon

After you've narrowed your travel window to a month or two, let's consider the phases of the moon. Your final assault on the summit will be made at night, beginning around midnight. It will be to your advantage to plan your trip so that this time will be immediately after a full moon. We did not need any additional illumination (flashlight, headlamp) while the moon was out.

Your climb to Gilman's Point (the hardest part, and the part done at night) will be done up a scree slope (more about scree later) on the east side of Kibo Peak. This is what you want to have illuminated by the moon. This means that the nights about five days after the full moon will be well illuminated from midnight until daybreak. Earlier than that, the moon is setting

Date of the Full Moon from 2002 through 2020											
	Jan	Feb	Mar	Apr	May	June	July	Aug	Sept	Oct	Nov	Dec
2002	28	27	28	27	26	24	24	22	21	21	20	19
2003	18	16	18	16	16	14	13	12	10	10	9	8
2004	7	6	6	5	4	3	2, 31	30	28	26	24	24
2005	25	24	25	24	23	22	21	19	18	17	16	15
2006	14	13	14	13	13	11	11	9	7	7	5	5
2007	3	2	3	2	2	1, 30	30	28	26	26	24	24
2008	22	21	21	20	20	18	18	16	15	14	13	12
2009	11	9	11	9	9	7	7	6	4	4	2	2, 31
2010	30	28	30	28	27	26	26	24	23	23	21	21
2011	19	18	19	18	17	15	15	13	12	12	10	10
2012	9	7	8	6	6	4	3	2, 31	30	29	28	28
2013	27	25	27	25	25	23	22	21	19	18	17	17
2014	16	14	16	15	14	13	12	10	9	8	6	6
2015	5	3	5	4	4	2	2, 31	29	28	27	25	25
2016	24	22	23	22	21	20	19	18	16	16	14	14
2017	12	11	12	11	10	9	9	7	6	5	4	3
2018	2, 31	-	2, 31	30	29	28	27	26	25	24	23	22
2019	21	19	21	19	18	17	16	115	14	13	12	12
2020	10	9	9	8	7	5	5	4	3	1, 31	30	30

The dates of the full moon from 2002 through 2020. Ascent of Mount Kilimanjaro is best if it is scheduled so that the peak is attained immediately after a full moon.

This information was supplied with permission by Chris Osburn of Seattle, Washington, at website http://www.lunaroutreach.org/phases/phases.cgi

behind Kibo Peak (in front of you) before daybreak. So the recommended lunar window is within a few days after the full moon.

If you follow the timetable outlined in this chapter, you will be climbing to Gilman's Point five days after you arrive at Kilimanjaro International Airport (JRO). If possible, arrange your trip so that the full moon occurs within these five days. You will enjoy the moon every night you are on the mountain.

To determine the date of the full moon from now until the year 2020, consult the table above. Your trip should still be several months off, so things are still pretty flexible. Once you've bought those plane tickets, you are locked in!

Itinerary designed to acclimate

In order to arrive in Africa ready to climb to the top, we stopped first in Europe and stayed at as high an elevation as we could. This accomplished two goals: acclimating as much as possible to altitude and getting over jet lag. We crossed seven time zones when flying to Europe, and two more flying on to Tanzania. And it is a long flight! There is no way we could have hit that mountain in anything like peak physical condition if we had just flown directly from North America to Amsterdam, then to JRO. And, as we have mentioned, you want to be in peak physical condition.

Here's what we did. We flew on Northwest Airlines from Minneapolis to Amsterdam nonstop on an overnight flight, arriving in Amsterdam around noon. Northwest Airlines flies from North America nonstop to Amsterdam (AMS; Schiphol Airport) from Atlanta (ATL), Boston (BOS), Chicago (O'Hare, ORD), Detroit (DTW), Houston (Inter-Continental, IAH), Los Angeles (LAX), Memphis (MEM), Miami (MIA), Minneapolis/ St. Paul (MSP), Montreal (YUL), Newark (EWR), New York (JFK), San Francisco (SFO), Seattle (SEA), Toronto (YYZ), and Washington (Dulles, IAD), although not necessarily on a daily basis. Northwest Airlines is particularly convenient because they are partners with Royal Dutch Airlines (KLM), who flies nonstop to JRO twice a week. But the flight from North America to AMS will be long, and the flight from AMS to JRO is about 9 1/2 hours. You should also be aware that airline schedules are constantly in a state of flux, so this information, while correct at the time of this writing, is subject to change.

From Amsterdam we took a KLM flight to Geneva, Switzerland, and spent the night at a hotel (the Hotel Strasbourg-Univers, Rue Jean-Jacques Pradier 10, phone 011-44-20-8840 6698, www.asiatravel.com/switzerland/geneve/strasbourg, about US$170 for a double room with breakfast) near the main train station (Gare de Cornavin). The next morning we took the train to Zermatt. Trains are expensive in Switzerland. Through our

Stephen with Mount Rosa behind him

travel agent at home, we bought Swiss Passes that saved us considerable money over regular fares. They also included 25 percent discounts on the cog railroad and cable cars we took above Zermatt. It was a lovely four-hour trip along the north shore of Lake Geneva up into the Swiss Alps. We had to change trains at the town of Brig, which was a pleasant one-hour stopover.

Zermatt is a quintessential Swiss alpine town, capped off by the Matterhorn that absolutely dominates the scenery up the valley. We stayed at a pleasant hotel that offered inspiring views of the Matterhorn. This was the Hotel Holiday (Mr. Martin Perren, proprietor), phone 011-41-27 967 12 03; FAX 27 967 50 14, www.hotelholiday.ch/. The hotel was renovated in the spring of 1997. We were picked up at the train station and taken to the hotel in something like an electric golf cart. There are no cars in Zermatt, a beautiful and expensive city. The Hotel Holiday cost us about US$130 per person per night with breakfast.

From Zermatt (5,315 feet; 1,620 meters), we took the cogwheel train up to Gornergrat (10,000 feet; 3,100 meters) for the day, took a cable car from there to Stockhorn (11,588 feet; 3,532 meters) and hiked around. We did not know it beforehand, but there is a hotel at Gornergrat (billed as "the highest hotel in the Alps") that may be a better place to stay than in Zermatt. It is

Susan having lunch in view of the Matterhorn

the Kulm Hotel Gornergrat, CH-3920 Zermatt, Switzerland, phone 011-41-27 966 64 00, FAX 27 966 64 04. You can check on their rates at <u>www.zermatt.ch/gornergrat.kulm</u>, but they include dinner, breakfast buffet, services, and taxes, and may be notably less expensive than most hotels in the village of Zermatt. This hotel is lovely and in spectacular surroundings, but it is isolated. The funicular railroad that runs from Zermatt to Gornergrat is expensive (even with a 25 percent Swiss Pass discount), so you should factor in an additional expense if you want to get around elsewhere.

The next day, from Zermatt, we took a cable car to the Little Matterhorn (Klein Matterhorn) and hiked around at 12,533 feet (3,820 meters). The scenery on both of these outings was simply spectacular! Late the following morning we took the train back to Geneva and flew to Amsterdam to catch the

KLM flight to JRO the next morning. We stayed at the Ibis Amsterdam Airport Hotel (Schipholweg 181, NL-1171 PK Badhoevedorp, The Netherlands, phone 31-20-502-5200, www.holland-hotels.com/ibisairport.html) at a cost of about US$100 for the two of us, without breakfast. This hotel is particularly convenient, with a shuttle bus picking you up and dropping you off at Schiphol Airport. They also run a bus downtown, if you have some time to go sightseeing in Amsterdam.

The flight from Amsterdam to JRO was more than an hour longer than the flight from Minneapolis to Amsterdam! By the time we got to JRO it was dark, but we were picked up by a driver from our hotel and driven about an hour and a half to Marangu.

This description is rather detailed, but this schedule had us arriving at the foot of Mount Kilimanjaro quite refreshed and somewhat acclimated to altitude. The two obvious things that this "pre-trip" takes are time and money, but if you have enough of both, it should serve you as well as it served us. When we plan to climb the mountain the next time (we are considering climbing the "Hard Way"), a change we may make is to go to Chamonix, France, rather than Zermatt. It's not quite as high (3,400 feet; 1,037 meters), but it is at the foot of Mount Blanc, it's a little closer to Geneva, and may be not quite as expensive as Zermatt. Some other European locations that have been recommended to us include Saas Fee (not far from Zermatt, with similar altitudes), Grindelwald in the Bernese Alps (and hike from there to Mönchsjochhütte at 3600 meters). In Italy, you could consider Alagna Valsesia (from there take the cable car to Punta Indren, 3200 meters, and from there the mountain huts of Rifugio Citta di Mantova and Rifugio Gnifetti, 3611 meters, relatively easy hikes), or Courmayeur in Val d'Aosta. Austria, in general, is less expensive, and Kühtai near Innsbruck is accessible, even in winter. Other Austrian regions to consider are the Stubai region and Zillertal, although they are not particularly high.

Flying into JRO is by far the most convenient, but your choice of airlines is somewhat limited. The only airlines that fly into that airport are Royal Dutch Airlines (KLM), Ethiopian Airlines and Air Tanzania. For us, KLM was the most convenient since we could fly nonstop to and from Amsterdam. It is possible to fly to some other city, Nairobi in Kenya, for example, and fly or take some other transportation to Marangu, but the distances in Africa tend to be greater and more difficult to accomplish than most people think. Also, you will need a Kenyan visa if you enter at Nairobi.

Once you have made these flight arrangements, then you are committed. You're going to climb Mount Kilimanjaro, and you know when you are going to do it. We even "counted down" the lunar cycles until our trip. Your exercise training is going full tilt, and you're getting more excited (and nervous). Don't forget to tend to details such as scheduling the vacation time off from your job, making arrangements for your abode to be looked after in your absence, and all those other items that need to be addressed whenever you are away from home.

Finding an outfitter

It will be necessary for you to make arrangements for getting up the mountain. It is required by Tanzanian law (Mount Kilimanjaro is a National Park) for you to have a licensed guide on the mountain. You will see that this law makes a lot of sense when you get there! You will also need places to sleep on the mountain, and food. As you will see, providing these services is a major part of the local economy in the Marangu area.

To begin this phase of making your arrangements, you have two basic choices. There are outfitters around the world to whom you can pay your money and they will take care of everything for you. You can probably work this through your travel agent, but some companies that we know of are listed here. There is no doubt that they will do a fine job, but we see some disadvantages. First, they have schedules to meet, and if your schedule fits their schedule, fine, but this could present a problem. Second, they have overhead and additional expenses (and let's face it, they need to make a profit in order to stay in business) that will be added to the cost of your trip. But if you would prefer to have someone else take care of your needs and take responsibility for planning the details of your trip, then this may be the way to go for you.

Stateside outfitters that we know of are:

Wilderness Travel
801 Allston Way
Berkeley, CA 94710 USA
800-368-2794

Mountain Madness
4218 S.W. Alaska St., Suite #206
Seattle, WA 98116 USA
800-328-5925

Overseas Adventure Travel
800-221-0814

Your other choice is to contact an outfitter in Tanzania. The list of outfitters we contacted is:

Marangu Hotel, Seamus Brice-Bennett, Proprietor
PO Box 40
Moshi, Tanzania (Africa)

Key's Hotel
Sindato Ndesamburo, Managing Director
PO Box 933
Moshi, Tanzania (Africa)
email: Keys@form-net.com

Trans Kibo Travels Ltd.,
Thomas E. Lyimo, Managing Director
PO Box 558
Moshi, Tanzania (Africa)

Kibo Hotel, Marina Stromvall, General Manager
PO Box 102
Marangu, Tanzania (Africa)
FAX 00255 55 51308

Tropicana Safari Tours,
Leonard K.B. Ndoro, Tour Manager
PO Box 884
Moshi, Tanzania (Africa)

Hoopoe Adventure Tours
Terri Rice, Marketing Executive
PO Box 2047, India Street
Arusha, Tanzania (Africa)
email: hoopoeuk@aol.com

After comparing services and prices, we settled on the Marangu Hotel. One of the reasons we made this choice was that we were impressed with the proprietor, Seamus Brice-Bennett. And we'll tell you that we were not disappointed when we finally had the opportunity to meet him in person. You can check out the website for the Marangu Hotel at www.maranguhotel.com.

What are you looking for in an outfitter? They will be responsible for guiding you up the mountain, making reservations at huts for you to sleep in along the route, carrying the bulk (and you will see that this term is well chosen) of your gear, as well as carrying and preparing your food. So you will need to contact either an international company or a Tanzanian outfitter and agree on services and prices.

An extra day?

Another variable that you will need to consider at this stage is how many days you can schedule for the climb. You will get a better idea later (see chapters 9 and 10), but we recommend planning for an extra day at Horombo Hut, elev. 12,200 feet. This is another one of those choices that will optimize your chances of making it to the top. It will add an extra day to your trip and increase your cost by about $100 per person.

On the following page is a graph of the days we spent on Mount Kilimanjaro plotted against altitude. When we got to the top we were assigned numbers. Our numbers meant that Susan was the 1,492nd person to reach Uhuru Peak in 1996, and I was the next.

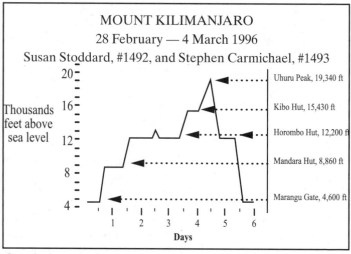

Graph showing the number of days on Mount Kilimanjaro plotted against altitude

Paperwork

In preparation for your trip, you will have some additional details to attend to that involve paperwork. Make sure your passport is valid for a period that extends at least a month past your return date from Tanzania. If it needs to be renewed, or it's even close, renew it. You will also need a visa. If you are a United States citizen, call the Embassy of The United Republic of Tanzania at (202) 939-6125 and they will mail you an application for a visa. You must call between 9:00 A.M. and noon, Eastern Time. Their address is The Embassy of the United Republic of Tanzania, 2139 R Street, NW, Washington, DC 20008. If you are a citizen of another country, you can visit their website at www.embassy.org/embassies/tz.html for the location of an Embassy near you.

The visa application is not trivial. The Embassy requires copies of your airline ticket and a letter from your banker, or some such responsible party, attesting to the fact that you have the resources to get to and *from* Tanzania. It will require a few weeks and $45 per application. You will have the choice of applying for a "single entry" or "multiple entry" visa. If you will be arriving and departing from JRO and staying within Tanzania, the single entry will do, but if you will be visiting Kenya or some other neighboring country and need to get back into Tanzania, you will need a multiple entry visa.

Another paperwork detail is money to take with you. Cash is fine, and American dollars are accepted just about anywhere in the region. (We recommend carrying much of your cash in small bills. You can expect to receive change in Tanzanian shillings and it is difficult, even impossible, to have it converted back to exportable currency when you are departing.) But we are not comfortable carrying much cash, so we went with traveler's checks. They worked fine, but it does involve a *lot* of extra busywork. We were always required to put lots of information on the back of *each* and *every* check, including name, address, and passport number. This gets old really fast! Another possibility is a credit card, such as Visa, MasterCard, American Express, etc. However, these are not accepted at many places, and those that do accept them tend to charge an additional 6 percent or so to cover their extra expenses. Nevertheless, a credit card is always a good backup for unanticipated expenses or emergencies. Be sure to check the expiration date and have a new card issued if necessary. Your credit card company will be all too happy to accommodate you.

By the way, how are those workouts going? Sweating every day? Good!

7 — Gearing up

As was mentioned in the last chapter, you can contract with your outfitter to provide your gear (this means that you rent it) or you bring it with you. We chose the latter option because that gave us some control over our situation, plus we now have the gear for other trips. (We did most of our shopping at REI. We were impressed with the variety of choices, quality of the merchandise, and, particularly, the knowledgeable salespeople. They were all experienced in using what they sold to us and this counted for a lot. Check out their website at www.rei.com for more details. Given the level of cleanliness possible on such a mountain in such an isolated place (what we mean here is the *lack* of cleanliness), you may prefer to maximize your hygienic environment. Also, many of the items are quite personal (like hiking boots; would you climb in someone else's boots?), so it makes a lot of sense to bring these with you.

Provided in appendix B is a complete list of gear that we brought with us, including medical items and food. But this list needs some amplification.

Start at your feet

Let's begin from the bottom up. To say that a well-broken-in pair of hiking boots is essential would be an understatement. This is probably the first purchase you will want to make, because proper breaking-in takes time. The key in this selection process is to find a sporting goods store that has a salesperson whom you can trust. The selection of boots is bewildering, and you need the best advice you can get. As a knowledgeable salesperson will tell you, the fit of your boot is more important for the trip down the mountain than for going up. The fit needs to be such that the deceleration pressure is on the top of your foot, not on the ends of your toes. And get advice on breaking-in, too. We first wore our boots for many hours while just walking around the house, or reading a book (not hiking). This gets the boot to fit around your foot better. Then start with longer and longer walks. Treat your boots with a water repellent, for even if you are climbing during the "dry" season, you will likely be crossing some streams and walking in mud. We both ended up with Raichle Spirit II boots and were very pleased with their performance.

While we're here, let's talk next about socks. It is well known by hikers that a polypropylene sock liner is advisable. (Make sure the liners are 100 percent polypropylene. Some other materials are available and apparently they do not work as well.) This thin sock "wicks" moisture (sweat) away from your feet and really improves their environment. A couple pairs of these liners come in handy, as you can use them on alternate days. Thick, comfortable socks come next. Keep in mind that it will be cold at the top. Look for socks made of virgin wool (higher oil content), or a wool synthetic blend. (An option, instead of the sock liner and thick sock, is to wear two pairs of thick socks, which some experienced hikers prefer.) It is a good idea to buy your boots and socks at the same time and use them together during the break-in period.

Something else you may consider while you're down here are inserts that go into the bottom of your boot. Spenco makes a good product. The company claims that Spenco's patented Polysorb® Replacement Insoles have been shown to provide superior shock absorption and energy return. This makes sense to us. The person from whom you bought your boots may have some specific recommendations, for there are several inserts on the market. We suggest ones that add extra cushioning between your feet and the ground. You are going to be pounding your feet across a lot of ground (a total of about 50 miles on the Tourist Route), and you will be happier if you can lessen the impact.

Sleeping gear

Sleeping bags are another major purchase. We were very happy with an REI brand. We recommend the "mummy" style of bags, probably down-filled, that are rated to 0°F. We have heard of recommendations of +10°F, which may be fine for you. Again, you need the advice of a knowledgeable salesperson. Sleeping bags come in different lengths, so be sure yours fits you well. Don't hesitate to climb into the bag in the store. It may feel a little strange, but a good salesperson will expect (even insist) that you do this. It is also a good idea to "break in" your sleeping bag. This really is more for your own training, rather than for the good of the bag. Sleeping in a mummy bag is quite different than a normal bed. For example, if you roll over, you don't roll over *in* the bag, you roll over *with* the bag. Sleep in your bag for several nights, even in your own bedroom, until you get used to nuances of being wrapped up like a mummy.

If you have decided to take the Marangu Route, you will not need a tent because you will be sleeping in huts. (If you are going by any other route, you will need to buy or rent a tent.) Sleeping platforms with "mats" are in the hut. We supplemented the cushioning and insulation factors by bringing along "self-inflating" air mattresses, also made by REI. These are nifty little rolls that expand and suck in air when you open the valve. They worked well, even at 15,430 feet. In the morning you open the valve and roll them up tightly.

Packs

Backpacks are another item. A large backpack is handy for getting your gear through airports, train stations, etc., to Africa. However, on the mountain we were astonished to see our porters put these backpacks into a plastic bag (protection from the rain), and then inside a burlap sack, and then put this on their head and take off up the mountain. As an aside, we need to tell you that they could maintain a much faster pace than we could! The point here is that the main container for your clothes and gear does not need to be a backpack. Anything that you can get to Africa, and that your porter can carry on his head, will do fine.

What you will need is a relatively small daypack. You will have ready access to all of your gear each and every morning, and every night. What you need during the day, you carry (remember, your porter is way ahead of you). For us this came down to carrying a camera, an extra roll of film, sunscreen, an extra article of warm clothing (a sweatshirt or sweater for when we stopped), lunch (which is supplied each morning), and a water bottle. Our water bottles were wrapped in an Aqua Sack jacket that came with straps to either put around us or to hang the bottle from our daypack. We always carried a Swiss Army knife, but this didn't add much to the bulk of our daypacks. We used JanSport packs with three compartments. The compartment next to our back was for the extra layer of clothing (it served as padding), camera gear was in the middle compartment (where it was best protected), and lunch was in the outer compartment.

Walking sticks

Next let's talk about walking sticks. You can go low-tech or high-tech. A slick product is the Super Makalu walking sticks made by Leki (named for Makalu, a mountain in the Himalayas, the fifth tallest mountain in the world, 27,766 feet; 8,156 meters). Surely there are many adequate products on the market, but this one was particularly good. For starters, they telescope out from three sections giving you two advantages: collapsed they are very compact for traveling, and they can be extended to any length you could want (this can vary on the trek; shorter for going up steep grades, longer for going downhill). Another nice feature is that they are spring-loaded, so the transmission of shock up your upper limbs is minimized. We used our poles almost constantly on Mount Kilimanjaro. They were essential for getting to the top and critical for getting back down. They took some of the strain and shock off the lower limbs and were

Susan demonstrating proper hiking attire: cap, sunglasses, water bottle, walking sticks, and hiking boots. Her porter is doing the real work behind her.

valuable for balance when walking over precarious terrain, through streams and mud, etc. The low-tech option is to get one or two wooden sticks. This may be better than nothing, but they could be more dangerous than nothing, too.

Clothes

The major item we're left with is clothes. Your wardrobe must be well planned in advance. As you've already guessed, layering is the trick here. You need to be prepared for hot (90°F) at the bottom, cold (below 0°F at the top, with a stiff wind), and everything (including rain) in between. Fortunately, at the Marangu Hotel there were people to check through our gear to see that we were adequately prepared.

From Marangu Gate up to Kibo Hut, it gets progressively colder. You will want to be dressed for hot weather and add layers as you go. Light nylon pants, made by REI, with legs that zipped off worked very well. A long-sleeved cotton T-shirt with cotton gloves covered the top at lower altitudes. You'll notice

59

that we are covering almost all of our skin; protection from the sun is important here. Carry a sweater or sweatshirt in your daypack to put on when you stop. It will be cooler and cooler at each stop.

Above Kibo Hut, you will need cold-weather gear. From the inside out, polypropylene long underwear works superbly. We used a product by Helly Hansen called LIFA™ that served us very well. They were not only our underwear, they were our pajamas at night, too. As you've guessed, it moves the perspiration away from the skin and keeps it dry. And you can count on perspiring!

Our next layer was a silk long-sleeved turtleneck shirt, followed by a heavy, long-sleeved turtleneck and another Helly Hansen product called a Furnace shirt. On the outside was a full parka. I wore a Columbia Williwaw parka. This garment has a "layered" design that is particularly effective for subzero skiing in Minnesota and worked well on top of Mount Kilimanjaro as well. Susan wore a Stearns windbreaker-type parka that served her well. On the bottom, over our LIFA™ underwear was a pair of Furnace pants, with insulated ski pants on the outside. Polypropylene sock liners and the warmest socks we could find covered our feet. Thermal glove liners and heavy-duty mittens (which are warmer than gloves) covered our hands. Our heads were covered with a silk balaclava and heavy winter hats. The balaclava is a relatively thin hood that covers your entire head and neck, save an opening for your eyes and nose. We used silk balaclavas from WinterSilks (800-648-7455) that worked very well and were easy to pack.

To see the path

Good eye protection is a must. Ski goggles or reflective sunglasses work well. They should give 100 percent UV protection. We then used a scarf over the remainder of the face. If you've been paying attention, you will notice that *every single* square inch of skin is covered. This is how we avoided frostbite and sunburn, which can happen very easily at the top of Mount Kilimanjaro.

You will need some sort of portable illumination just to operate around the huts at night, going to the latrine, etc. What works particularly well is a dive light, rather than an ordinary flashlight. A dive light is a flashlight designed to work underwater. They can be found at any dive store that sells gear to SCUBA divers. A dive light is more rugged, and of course waterproof, when compared to a flashlight. They come in all sizes, from very compact to huge. Ikelite makes several sizes, including some great compact lights. Their PCa Lite is incredibly compact. Another choice is the brightness of the bulb. Physical laws dictate that the brighter bulbs (and Ikelite has some amazingly bright bulbs) run down the batteries faster. We would recommend a bulb of adequate brightness for you, with some extra batteries. Put in fresh batteries before you leave Kibo Hut.

A headlamp may be even more useful because your hands are free for other chores. This can be handling your walking sticks when going up The Snake in the dark (if it's not a full moon) or taking care of business in the latrine. The premier maker of headlamps appears to be Petzl. They make a compact, rugged device that fits comfortably. The beam can be adjusted from flood to spot. So the choice is yours as to your illumination, but you will need a dive light and/or a headlamp.

Diet at altitude

What are you going to eat on the mountain? It probably doesn't matter a great deal whether you go up the "tourist" route, with the small villages of A-frame huts where you spend the night, or go up one of the other routes, where you sleep in tents. Unless you bring high-tech, backpackers' dehydrated food with you, chances are very high that you will be relying on the local folks to choose, carry, and cook your food on the mountain. It was our experience in Tanzania, both on the mountain and later on a camping safari, that the food was pretty much the same from day to day (see A Hiker's Diary, chapter 1). Breakfast was tea, juice, porridge, eggs, and usually a fatty meat. Lunch on the mountain was packed in a paper sack and carried in our daypacks; we ate when we chose. This consisted of edibles such as boiled eggs, cheese and butter sandwiches, tomatoes, and fruit. The local small bananas were delicious; the oranges, which looked more like limes, were tart. You may want to bring some of your favorite snacks to supplement the lunch. Dinner was, first and always, soup! Largely to get fluids into us, but it was always delicious. We found out later that it was made from packages of Knorr dehydrated soup. The second course was carbohydrate (rice, pasta, or potatoes), usually fried, with well-cooked, pan-fried vegetables (carrots, cabbage...) and a "sauce," which usually contained some form of canned meat. Actually, this stuff was pretty tasty. Of course, walking all day and building a healthy appetite surely didn't hurt. Dessert was usually some form of canned seasoned fruit or fruit mixture; again, very tasty. Keep in mind that menus will differ depending on your particular cook, available food, the size of your group, and the facilities available (or not) for cooking on any certain day.

Another thing to think about is flatulence. With decreased atmospheric pressure, digestive gas expands, and flatulence may increase. So select foods that are least likely to cause gas in your individual system.

Looking at this diet, you may have noticed that it is quite high in carbohydrates. This is true, and there is logic to it. When you eat, you require oxygen to metabolize or "burn" the food. Carbohydrates provide 4 Kcal of energy for each gram metabolized; that metabolism requires one molecule of oxygen (O_2) to form one molecule of carbon dioxide (CO_2). This ratio of carbon dioxide output to oxygen utilization is the "respiratory quotient;" for carbohydrates it equals 1.0. This is considered to be very efficient. Protein also provides 4 Kcal of energy per gram, but yields 8 molecules of carbon dioxide for every 10 molecules of oxygen (respiratory quotient of 0.8). Fat provides 9 Kcalories per gram, but with a respiratory quotient of 0.7. This means

A porter bringing firewood to Horombo Huts. All of our food was cooked over wood fires.

that the metabolic processes for protein and fat are less efficient, requiring more oxygen than an equivalent amount of carbohydrates. Carbohydrate metabolism requires relatively less oxygen, and this is important when oxygen is at a premium. (A five-day study on Mount Kilimanjaro of 16 people who ate native foods and self-selected snacks, found an average consumption of 56 percent carbohydrates, 16 percent protein, and 28 percent fat, yielding 1488 Kcalories per day. This was combined with two liters of fluid. There was a considerable range among the individual climbers.)

If you have a slightly touchy stomach or just want to stack the deck in your favor as much as possible, you may want to bring along some "favorite" energy-rich foods that you know you like and that sit well in your digestive system. There are many low-fat energy bars that are high in protein and carbohydrate, such as Power Bars, Cliff Bars, Met-Rex, and others. We also made our own version of trail mix with Wheat Chex, Rice Chex, mini Shredded Wheat, small pretzels, dried cranberries, apricots, figs, dates, and apples, carob-covered raisins, and a few cashews. You can mix up anything that sounds good to you. The trick is to have high complex carbohydrates, low fat, and a few goodies that will encourage you to eat it! We packed a cup or two into several Zip-lock bags and stuffed them in all the nooks and crannies of our luggage. None came home! Other things you might take, depending on your personal tastes: peanut butter, powdered skim milk, instant oatmeal, etc. Remember, also, that your digestive system will be competing with your lungs for the little oxygen there is, so rest after eating and eat smaller, more frequent meals. (At 18,000 feet, 50 percent of your sea level work capacity is lost, so you will need all the calories you can get to provide the needed energy.)

We also gave ourselves a little boost with the contents of our water bottles. We purified our water with iodine purification tablets; perhaps not necessary, but it surely didn't hurt. To make the water more palatable, we added powdered Gatorade at half the recommended concentration (6 to 8 percent sugar, or 1/2 teaspoon per 1/2 cup) or a powdered drink and Equal. The Gatorade worked best, because the sugar was already included, and that in itself provided energy. (An alternative is a hand-pumped water filter that avoids the iodine taste. Having water as palatable as possible is important when forcing yourself to drink large quantities of fluids to stay hydrated.)

Another thing that will help, and in retrospect is very highly recommended on the day you attempt the summit, is a carbohydrate powder added to your water. Carbohydrates are absorbed into the bloodstream as simple sugars, such as glucose, that are readily metabolized for energy. The body stores carbohydrates in the form of glycogen, which is broken down into glucose as needed by the body. To have glucose available is to have energy; to have glycogen available is to have reserves of energy.

To be glycogen-depleted is to have no reserves. You can use the Gatorade powder, or you can find something in your local nutrition store. The carbohydrate will give you a little energy and the fluid will fight dehydration. You also may wish to add glucose polymers such as Polycose® (20 to 25 percent

Susan with Protas and Isadori at Gilman's Point

solutions may be needed for glycogen replacement). I believe this is the one mistake we made on the mountain. We had the carbohydrate powder but did not add it to our water; we didn't drink as much as we should have, partly because our bottles froze, even though they were insulated. We were lucky and still reached the summit, but we were severely glycogen-depleted and dehydrated when we finished, which could have been at least partially avoided. When you don't sleep that night at Kibo Hut at 15,500 feet, as you worry about starting for the top at midnight, your logic is not all it is at sea level. So make a deal with yourself before you leave Kibo Hut: Keep your water bottle under your parka in your sleeping bag during the night at Kibo Hut so it won't freeze, keep the bottle full of carbohydrate-supplemented fluid, and *drink it.*

Personal items

As the heading says, this is personal. But we can share with you some of the personal items that helped us on our trip. There is some down time at the huts, but there is not much privacy; you may be sharing a cozy hut with one or more strangers. We each brought a paperback book, but didn't read much. We like to play cards, and we did that almost every day. Listening to your favorite music on a portable cassette or compact disc player may help you retain your center or help you to drift off to sleep at night.

Be sure to include some of your personal favorite items to occupy your time. Getting excessively anxious about the task ahead of you will be counterproductive.

Cleanliness

This may seem to be a bit of an oxymoron, considering the primitive conditions on the mountain, but there are a few things you can do to make life a trifle more comfortable. First, bandannas. These can be used for handkerchiefs, washcloths, towels, or tied around your neck, damp or dry, to keep you cool or warm, respectively. Bring several. Soap, preferably something that rinses off easily in cold water. At least at the camps on the Marangu Route there is cold running water, and washing your hands and face can significantly improve your attitude. A small towel can soak up that cold water better than your bandanna. Those Wet Ones, like parents use with babies, are surely useful, particularly during the day, or if you are having bowel difficulties, but cannot replace cold water and soap in the evening! A toothbrush and toothpaste are significantly better than the little disposable flavored pink foam sponge on a stick. The idea sounded great; the experience was not rewarding! Zip-lock plastic bags: to keep things organized; to keep clean things clean and dirty things away from the clean ones. For what they weigh, you can't have too many of them!

Now that you're all geared up, let's consider taking care of your health needs.

8 — Medical considerations

Tropical diseases and vaccinations

Recommendations on vaccinations change continually as epidemics wax and wane, so you must get the current recommendations. Consult a physician or Public Health Office that has the latest publication of the Centers for Disease Control and Prevention (CDC; website www.cdc.gov) or the World Health Organization (WHO; website www.who.int). Some vaccinations are "required," some are "recommended." Get them all.

Any knowledgeable world traveler is protected against hepatitis A. The vaccination regimen requires two shots, six months apart, so you should begin this sooner rather than later. Hepatitis B is recommended only for those in the medical profession or missionaries, but your physician may recommend it. You need to be vaccinated against typhoid within the last five years. There is a well-tolerated oral vaccine available for typhoid. This part of Africa is usually within the "meningitis belt" so, depending on the current CDC report, meningococcal vaccine is recommended. Your polio vaccine, either oral or by injection, should be current within the past five years; tetanus within five years (don't get this one more often, as it may trigger a bad reaction); yellow fever within ten years; and finally your MMR (measles, mumps, rubella) should have been completed years ago, but make sure it was. The vaccination for cholera has not proven to be very effective, so we cannot recommend it.

Take your vaccination record with you, including proof of protection against yellow fever. Travel books that we read said it was no longer necessary to show this documentation, but our vaccination records were carefully checked, even before we had to show our passports, at JRO.

It is imperative that you be protected against tropical diseases. Malaria is endemic in equatorial Africa, and since that is where Mount Kilimanjaro is located, you must provide for protection from this. Malaria is a very serious (life threatening) disease that is difficult to treat, but relatively easy to prevent with prophylactic medication. Consult your physician; he or she may prescribe Lariam as the drug of choice. It is supplied as a tablet and it is important to take the tablet with food, drinking at least eight ounces of water with it. You will be instructed to take this drug a week before you arrive in Africa, every week you are there, and for four weeks after you return home. (Lariam is the brand name of mefloquine HCl distributed by Hoffman-LaRoche. The usual dose is 250 mg taken once a week. There is some controversy about Lariam. It has apparently triggered psychotic episodes, or at least strange behavior, in some patients.)

Another drug that may be recommended to you is Malarone. This is a fixed-dose combination of the antimalarial agents atovaquone (250 mg.) and proguanil hydrochloride (100 mg.) made by Glaxo Wellcome. Malarone should be taken at the same time every day, beginning a day or two before entering an area with malaria, and continuing for 7 days after returning home. Since Malarone is taken daily (Larium is taken once a week), it is more expensive than Larium, but Malarone may be more suitable for some patients. At the low dosage for malaria prophylaxis, there are rarely any reported side effects, although with higher doses used for treating malaria, side effects include nausea, diarrhea, headache, and dizziness.

Others recommend a mixture of chloroquine and nivaquine for malaria prophylaxis. It is said that you cannot catch malaria above about 9,000 feet on Mount Kilimanjaro (because the insects that transmit it don't live above that altitude) but you must be careful at lower altitudes, particularly if you visit the coast where the strains of malaria can be especially virulent.

With the AIDS epidemic in parts of Africa, we did not want to take a chance on the condition of local medical equipment, especially syringes and needles. We took some sterile ones with us and thankfully did not need them. Our rationale was to have them in case we needed an injection of a snake antivenom (we never saw a snake) or some unforeseen emergency. You may need a prescription from your physician to obtain these supplies at a drug store.

Altitude sickness

Acute mountain sickness (AMS) is the mildest form of altitude sickness and may be considered simply a failure to acclimatize. The failing, which is reversible, is in the way the body handles pH, salt, and water. Most individuals will have some symptoms of AMS ascending Mount Kilimanjaro. Others will have the same symptoms when they fly to a ski resort in Colorado, at around 8,000 feet of altitude. There are no sure ways to know the degree to which you will suffer from AMS, as it seems to be largely genetically controlled. Further, individuals who go to altitude may have different symptoms at different times. There is nothing, other than acclimatization, that you can do to minimize altitude sickness. Acclimatization involves an interplay among 1) rate of ascent, 2) altitude, 3) intensity of work and ventilation, and 4) food and water intake.

Physical fitness is no guarantee that AMS will not affect you; what can be said is that if you are physically fit, you will exert less energy in your efforts at altitude. A mild form of AMS feels like a hangover, including headache (which can usually be treated by an over-the-counter analgesic), edema (swelling, which results from accumulation of fluid within tissues) of the hands and feet, difficulty sleeping, malaise, mild nausea and/or loss of appetite, and, with increasing severity, vomiting. The difficulty sleeping may be caused in part by alterations in breathing (periodic breathing pattern) during sleep at altitude. For this reason, taking sleeping pills to facilitate sleep is not recommended, as sleeping pills generally decrease the breathing rate even further. One drug for altitude illness, Diamox® (see below), is thought to exert part of its effect by increasing breathing rate during sleep.

Another physiologic effect of altitude is to cause diuresis (increased output of urine). Add to this the dry mountain air that quickly removes moisture from your breath (which has increased in rate), plus perspiration, and dehydration becomes a serious threat to your sense of well-being. Additionally, dehydration results in fatigue, and you will be feeling enough of this without any extenuating factors! Thus, one of the most important things that you can do to keep yourself feeling better and increase your chances of making it to the top is to *DRINK*. We have mentioned this before (and we will mention it again), but your fluid intake should be four to five liters per day. You don't have to measure this (the truth is, it would be difficult), but you can tell by your urine output. Urine flow should be "clear and copious"; dark, concentrated urine is a sure sign you are not drinking enough. Don't wait until you're thirsty; by that time you are already dehydrated. Think of thirst as the way your body tells you it's dehydrated. Plan consistent, regular stops for small drinks, and you will feel much better.

The commonly used drug for altitude sickness is acetazolamide (Diamox®). However, as you would suspect, it does have side effects (such as tingling sensations and alterations in taste) that can be rather unpleasant.

The important part of how Diamox® works is that the conversion of carbonic acid to carbon dioxide and water ($H_2CO_3 = CO_2 + H_2O$) is catalyzed by carbonic anhydrase, and if you can slow down this enzyme (using a carbonic anhydrase inhibitor, which is what Diamox® is), you can retain carbonic acid and keep the buffering system within your body in balance.

If you want to have Diamox® as insurance against altitude sickness, you must get a prescription from your physician. The dosage for acute mountain sickness is not universally agreed upon. The Physician's Desk Reference (PDR, a handbook of

Susan at the latrine at Horombo Huts. Kibo Peak is in the background.

pharmaceuticals) suggests 500 mg to 1000 mg daily, using divided doses or sustained-release capsules. However, some people experience side effects from this dosage, so you and your physician may want to consider a lower dose. One suggestion is to take half of a tablet (125 mg) in the morning and in the afternoon each day during your ascent. This is a relatively small dose, but it needs to be spread out because the effect of the enzyme inhibition wears off in 8 to 10 hours. It is usually advised to initiate dosing 24 to 48 hours before ascent and continue for 48 hours while at altitude or longer as needed to control symptoms. What we would do if we were going to take Diamox® on Mount Kilimanjaro is to take 125 mg the evening of our arrival at Horombo Hut, continuing with morning and evening doses our next day at Horombo, on the day to Kibo Hut, the morning (night) we start for the top, and perhaps one last dose upon our return to Horombo. This is probably the closest you can get to minimizing your chances of getting serious altitude sickness without experiencing unpleasant side effects.

We recommend that you test this dosage sometime when you are home, under the guidance of your physician, several weeks before you leave for Africa. See for yourself what the side effects feel like. Some individuals experience rare, severe side effects; for example, an allergic (anaphylactic) reaction is possible, since some people are allergic to sulfa drugs and Diamox® is a sulfonamide.

This discussion has dealt with the use of Diamox® to *prevent* altitude sickness. As a *treatment* for altitude sickness, Diamox® can be used in a dose of 250 mg every 8 to 12 hours for 48 hours. In addition, increase oral fluids (Diamox® is a diuretic and your urine output will increase!) and consider taking a rest day, or even descending. We hope this will not be necessary.

Whereas any form of altitude sickness is unpleasant (the most common being headache and nausea), there are forms that are very serious, and people have died on Mount Kilimanjaro from complications of altitude sickness. Of particular concern are *High Altitude Pulmonary Edema* (HAPE) and *High Altitude Cerebral Edema* (HACE).

HAPE is a derangement in the lungs caused by fluid accumulating within the pulmonary tissues. This makes the exchange of oxygen and carbon dioxide progressively more difficult, resulting in a lack of oxygen. Symptoms can come on gradually or relatively quickly, but you need to know what to look for, not only in yourself, but in your climbing partner(s) as well. Many people will have only a persistent dry cough; this may be the only initial sign of developing HAPE. Coughing up blood is definitely an advanced and serious sign. You should be able to catch your breath at rest.

HACE is a condition whereby fluid accumulates in the brain. The problem here is that the brain is encased within the rigid skull, and there is no room for expansion. This means that pressure within the skull will increase if the brain tissue starts to swell. Early warning signs are balance problems (that is, inability to walk a straight line). Balance problems may proceed to unconsciousness, then death.

The most important treatment of HAPE, HACE, and severe AMS is immediate descent! Of course, the best course of action is to prevent them by acclimatization in the first place. By this we mean ascending at a rate that allows your body to adjust to the new physiologic demands that you are putting on it. For more information about altitude sickness, check out www.high-altitude-medicine.com and www.princeton.edu/~oa/index.shtml.

A book that we strongly recommend if you have an interest in altitude sickness is *High Altitude Illness and Wellness: Beyond the Basics* by Charles S. Houston, M.D., who is widely regarded as the "guru" of mountain sickness. This book is available from ICS Books, Inc.; see References for ordering details. Among his many credentials, he led the first American expedition to K2 (at 28,251 feet) in 1938. I have had the pleasure of talking with Dr. Houston and he is a very impressive gentleman! We have something in common besides an interest in climbing, in that both he and I (Stephen) have published articles in *Scientific American*. Another authoritative source of information is an article by Peter Hackett and Robert Roach that was published recently ("High-altitude illness," *New England Journal of Medicine* Vol. 345, No. 2, pp. 107-114, 2001).

Of course, you have noticed that edema is the common element in these serious complications. You can expect some minor edema (swelling) in your hands and feet as a normal consequence of ascending to such an altitude. What is important here is to drink plenty of fluids, avoid overexertion, and to "climb high and sleep low." By this we mean to spend the late part of your hike moving to a high altitude, but going to a lower altitude to spend the night.

One "rule of thumb" that may work for you is to always breathe through your nose on the climb up. It's not the breathing through the nose that's important, but rather it's the climbing slowly enough to permit continuous nasal respiration. If you're exerting yourself to where you have to breathe through your mouth, you're climbing too fast. This advice works below Kibo Hut. If you were to take the scree slope up to Gilman's Point while only breathing through your nose, you would die of old age before you reached the top! This piece of territory is affectionately known as The Snake because you're constantly switching back and forth across the hill in a serpentine fashion (see p. 37, map of the Marangu Trail route). The distance up The Snake from Kibo Hut is "only" about 3,000 feet, approximately equivalent to laying nine Empire State Buildings end-to-end and climbing away. The bad news is that you cover about 11,000 feet (about two miles) to achieve that vertical gain; that's an incline of 27 percent. The really bad news is that, at Kibo Hut (15,000 feet above sea level), the oxygen density is only about one-half that found in New York City, and you're just starting there.

The other two pieces of advice that we can offer involve spending time at altitude to acclimatize. A pre-trip to places of higher altitude in the Alps is useful for acclimatization, but is especially helpful in coping with jet lag. The other good idea is to stay an extra day at Horombo Hut. We hiked up to the foot of Mawenzi and enjoyed a spectacular view of Kibo Peak across The Saddle on our "free" day. This will add to the cost of your hike (about $100 for two people) but it could make the difference between making it to the top, or not. We cannot overemphasize the importance of proper acclimatization as a key to success in reaching the summit. Even very fit persons may experience debilitating altitude sickness if they are not acclimatized. There is currently no way to predict reliably who will or will not be susceptible to altitude sickness. People who have experienced HAPE may be at a higher risk to experience HAPE again. However, if you are not properly acclimatized, you will be inviting trouble.

Drugs

One of the most common drugs ingested worldwide is caffeine. If you are a heavy coffee drinker, you may be a potential victim of "caffeine withdrawal headache" if you are deprived of your favorite brew for even a single day. This can be very severe, even incapacitating, when trying to climb a mountain. If this could be a problem for you, please choose one of these three options: 1) wean yourself off coffee (or your caffeine source of choice) over a period of several weeks before you leave for Africa, 2) take twice as much instant coffee as you'll need for your trip, give half to your porters as a gift (instant coffee seems to be something of a luxury item, even though coffee is grown in the region) and ask them to make you coffee each morning with the remaining half, or 3) buy caffeine tablets at a drug store, and take one or two tablets (depending on the severity of your addiction) each morning when you are unable to get your usual morning dose.

If caffeine isn't in first place, then ethanol (alcohol) is probably the most commonly ingested drug. A point about alcohol to keep in mind: it is a diuretic. Recall that diuresis increases with altitude, and altitude sickness is associated with dehydration, so be *very sparing* with alcohol ingestion on Mount Kilimanjaro.

We took some other drugs with us. Headache remedies: Ibuprofen (Advil®) acetaminophen (Tylenol®), or aspirin. Bring what works best for you and plenty of it. Expect to get a headache at altitude. Sleeping pills or melatonin for sleeping on the plane and resetting your "clock" due to the time zones you'll be flying over. (Remember that sleeping pills are *not* recommended at altitude.) It's your choice if it's over-the-counter (OTC) or prescription; whatever works. And, of course, if you are on any type of prescription medication, bring plenty with you.

Cough drops or lozenges could probably be called drugs, so we'll include them here. We brought bags and bags of Ricola "natural herb" cough drops (hard candy may do) to suck on, and we used or gave away every single one. At altitude, the air is really dry, so cough drops were particularly welcome. We shared them with our guides, who were very appreciative. A warning here. The dryness will dehydrate you quickly, so be sure to drink frequently. Don't let the cough drops mask your impending dehydration. Drink plenty!

Skin care

As you climb higher, there is less atmosphere to shield you from the ultraviolet rays of the sun. Thus, adequate protection from sunburn is required, regardless of your skin color. We saw several sorry people with uncomfortable sunburns. A sunscreen with a high sun protection factor (SPF) number is needed. An SPF of 30 is good, 50 may be a little better. Banana Boat has an SPF 50 Maximum Sunblock which you should consider if you're pale or burn easily. We also used a lip balm by Banana Boat with an SPF of 30.

The cold, dry air together with the wind can also severely dry or chap your skin, and you may wish to protect yourself or need to treat yourself. Any high quality moisturizer for "dry skin" would help. You might also want to include some Mentholatum to treat any skin that does become chapped or wind burned, especially around your nose and mouth.

Insects are a significant potential problem, at least at lower altitudes. A repellent with a high percentage of DEET (N,N-di-ethyl-meta-toluamide) works best. In case you do have itchy bites, or rashes, or similar problems, cortisone ointment (0.5 percent or 1 percent) is available OTC. A wide-spectrum antibiotic ointment is also available OTC. Don't let scratches become infected!

Eye care

We mentioned in the previous chapter that you must protect your eyes. This is as important as protecting your skin from the harmful effects of the sun and dry wind. We recommended that you include sunglasses or goggles that provided 100 percent blockage of UV rays.

People who use corrective lenses, particularly contact lens wearers, have special concerns on Mount Kilimanjaro — cleanliness and dry air. If you are careful in washing your hands before handling your lenses, you may wish to try wearing them up to Horombo Hut (12,500 feet). We would not recommend wearing contact lenses above Horombo, as the air becomes too dry. Rather, use prescription glasses, preferably with lenses that darken, so they can double as sunglasses. Also, bring along some eyedrops to help combat the dryness.

Foot care

Perhaps the last, but certainly not the least, member of your health care team that you assemble is a podiatrist (graduate of a School of Podiatry with a DPM [Doctor of Podiatric Medicine] degree. If you don't know where to look for a podiatrist, try the Yellow Pages of your phone book under Physicians & Surgeons-Podiatric.) Your podiatrist, sometimes casually referred to as a foot doctor, is the best-qualified person to keep your feet happy, and you will need happy feet to get to the top of Mount Kilimanjaro, not to mention down. If you have had problems with your feet, getting evaluated by your podiatrist is that much more critical. For example, if you have a problem with ingrown toenails, these can be treated with a procedure called a P&A, whereby your podiatrist eliminates the extra toenail on the sides with phenol and alcohol.

We were able to get advice from our podiatrist that minimized the number of blisters we got, as well as how to deal with the ones we did get. This turned out to be very important. We know of people who failed to reach the summit of Mount Kilimanjaro because their feet were bleeding. With the proper care, as recommended by your podiatrist, this won't happen to you.

Our podiatrist emphasized preventive treatment for blisters. Keeping our feet dry was important, and the polypropylene liners inside our socks played a major role in this. Small bundles of lamb's wool (available at a drug store) put between toes that are prone to blisters helps. If you find that your boots are rubbing a particular spot on your foot, you can protect it by putting Moleskin directly on the skin. Moleskin is an adhesive material that will eliminate friction over the troubled spot.

If you get small blisters that are not very painful, leave them alone. Large blisters may be lanced to relieve the pain, but you *must* be very careful to avoid infection! Sterilize the area with an alcohol wipe, and sterilize the needle either by holding it in the flame of a match or thoroughly wiping it with alcohol. Insert the needle into the edge of the blister, being careful not to injure underlying tissue. Compress the blister to express all of the fluid possible. Then put a dab of antibacterial ointment over the pinhole and apply a sterile bandage. An alternative would be to cover the area with New-Skin Liquid Bandage. It is imperative that you keep the site of broken skin sterile and covered. An infection would not only spoil your trip, but having your foot amputated is not out of the realm of possibility!

Feminine concerns

If you are trying to get pregnant, we would suggest that you postpone your attempt at climbing Mount Kilimanjaro, perhaps until your children are in high school. We don't know of any studies to back up our suggestion, but the primitive conditions and lack of oxygen at altitude cannot be good for a fetus.

Our other recommendation would be to coordinate your climb with your menstrual cycle. Easier said than done, particularly with the physical and emotional stresses of the climb. Since you will be planning your climb months in advance, one suggestion is to use birth control pills to regulate your cycle. This, however, should be done only in consultation with your physician. Although there is no evidence that birth control pills cause blood clots at altitude, this is something that should be discussed. Even if you believe that you will not be menstruating on the mountain, be prepared, and carry the smallest tampon or napkin that will work for you. Also, not knowing where you may need this, carry a good supply of small, zip-lock bags. If you are not at a camp with trash bins, all trash must be carried with you off the mountain.

Bowel habits

Sorry about this, but we saw plenty of evidence that folks had problems with their bowels on Mount Kilimanjaro. We took two tablets of bismuth subsalicylate (Pepto-Bismol, or its generic equivalent) with each and every meal and before going to bed. This helped, but did not solve all problems. Imodium A-D (loperamide hydrochloride) is an effective OTC antidiarrheal medication. Bring whatever works best for you. If you've never had a need for this type of medication, bring some along anyway. If you do develop what is called "traveler's diarrhea" (and you won't be alone!), be sure to drink plenty of safe liquids to avoid dehydration. Safe fluids would include bottled drinks (in their original containers) and coffee or tea (served steaming hot). Of these choices, you will find hot tea to be the most plentiful on Mount Kilimanjaro.

Impatiens kilimanjari

If you are unfortunate enough to come down with a *serious* case of diarrhea, you will abort your climb. This will be an easy decision; the cramps and malaise will decide for you. You now must turn your attention to dealing with loss of fluid and electrolyte imbalance that will be threatening your health, even your life. If carbonated water in its original container is available, use it, it's safe. If this is not available, use water that has been boiled for at least 15 minutes (longer if you're at altitude) and cooled down under hygienic conditions. To each liter (quart) of water, carbonated or boiled, add 1/2 teaspoon of table salt (sodium chloride), 1/2 teaspoon of baking soda (sodium bicarbonate), and 4 tablespoons of regular sugar (sucrose). Drink as much of this as you can tolerate.

If constipation is a problem for you, bring something along to deal with it. If incontinence is a problem, or a potential problem, bring some Depends incontinence products or similar undergarments with you. As far as we know, Depends incontinence products are not available in Africa.

You will need to bring your own toilet paper. Bring your favorite and bring more than enough; don't count on any being available on Mount Kilimanjaro.

9 — On the mountain

Time

First of all, take a waterproof watch that is reliable. For good measure, have new batteries installed. You will need to know what time it is in contexts such as "dinner will be served in 20 minutes," or "we will leave at 6:30." But you need to be a little careful with this latter context. There are two ways to tell time. We are accustomed to beginning the day in the middle of the night (we don't call it midnight for nothing) and usually start the numbers over again at noon. In "Tanzanian time" they start the day around daybreak, calling it 1:00 (that's 6 A.M. to us) and start over again at sundown (6 P.M. to us). This makes just as much sense as what we are used to, but you need to be clear which time frame your guide is using.

We experienced some confusion at Kibo Hut. Our guide told us to go to bed and he would get us at midnight to begin the final assault. Clear enough. Some other people were told by their guide to go to bed and he would get them at 6 o'clock. You can see where this could be confusing. Their guide came at the same time our guide did!

On a related note, you will notice something interesting at mid-day (noon or 6 o'clock, depending on your time reference). Because you are so close to the equator, your shadow almost completely disappears under your feet! For those of us who live well up into the Northern Hemisphere, this is an unusual observation.

Language

The native language in the region of Mount Kilimanjaro is Kiswahili, often referred to as Swahili. Compared to English (which is quite irregular), Swahili is a regular language that is relatively easy to learn. However, you are probably not into this undertaking for the linguistic experience, so you may not have the time and energy to devote to learning another language. If you are so inclined, a very handy book that will take you a long way is the *Swahili Phrasebook* published by Lonely Planet (see p. 104, References). The basics of the language are explained in a straightforward and useful manner. We strongly recommend at least adding a few phrases to your repertoire.

pole pole

Pronounced "po-lay po-lay," this means "slowly." This is the phrase that you will hear and use repeatedly. The context will be to describe your pace up Mount Kilimanjaro. This is the pace that you will maintain for several days, so come to love pole pole. An interesting point is that one may assume that it literally means "slowly, slowly," but that is not the case. *Pole* means "I'm sorry" as a consolation, rather than an apology.

hakuna matata

The reason this may sound familiar to you is that a musical number from the Disney movie The Lion King is named "Hakuna Matata." This is the second most useful phrase you will use. It means "no problem." This is your response when your guide asks you how you are doing. It is an important part of his job to assess your condition at altitude, and as long as you can convince him that you are having no problem, he will let you continue upwards. Call it a reality check.

jambo

This is the short form of "hello." The response is jambo. As you pass people on the route, this is the greeting that is consistently exchanged. There are many forms of greetings in Swahili, and they are an integral part of the culture, but if you use a more expanded greeting, you are likely to get a response that you can't understand. If you say jambo, a native may assume that you are a tourist from out of town who is in Tanzania to climb Mount Kilimanjaro. This will be a safe assumption.

mama

If you are a "mature" woman, this is how you will be addressed. It is a term of respect that would translate as madam, but it literally means "mother."

bibi

If you are a young woman, you may be addressed this way, with no disrespect intended. It would loosely translate as "miss."

papa

Similar to mama, this is a term of respect for a "mature" man.

bwana

This is another term by which men may be addressed. It is a term of respect that would translate as "sir."

asante sana

"Thank you very much." This phrase always comes in handy.

hatari

"Danger." If you see this on a sign, take the hint.

A few Swahili proverbs:

haba na haba hujaza kibaba

"Little and little fill the measure." You can shorten this to haba na haba.

haraka haraka haina baraka

"(In) hurry, hurry, there is no blessing."

pole pole ndiyo mwendo

"Slowly is indeed the (proper) path."

kawia ufike

"Be late (but) get there."

shauku nyingi huondoa maarifa

"Intense desire removes intelligence."

All of these proverbs relate to your getting up Mount Kilimanjaro. You can impress your guides by mumbling these to yourself, and it may help you to focus on your uphill struggle!

Stephen on our first day on the mountain, walking through the forest zone

Hiking techniques

Up to Kibo Hut there is nothing special about the hiking techniques required. Put one foot in front of the other. Walking sticks come in handy to steady yourself over uneven or muddy terrain and to take some of the stress off of your lower limbs. This part is quite enjoyable.

Above Kibo Hut, all the rules change. As we mentioned, this part will be begun at night, around midnight. From what we had read, we expected frozen scree; theoretically, one of the reasons you climb this part of the mountain at night is that it's easier to walk on scree when it's frozen. Wrong! First of all, what is scree? It is very loose and irregular gravel. Lots of dust, lots of little rocks, lots of big rocks. It's really miserable stuff to try to climb up through. And it wasn't frozen! Perhaps due to global warming, the ice cap on top of Mount Kilimanjaro has receded, leaving virtually no moisture on the approach to Gilman's Point. It has been reported that 82 percent of the ice cover on Mount Kilimanjaro has been lost since it was first mapped in 1912 and that the famous "Snows of Kilimanjaro" may disappear in 10 to 20 years. The result for us was that the scree was loose and unsteady. Every foothold up the mountain threatens to collapse under your foot, sending you two steps downhill. As you can appreciate, this makes for slow going. The trick is to plant your leading foot as securely as possible to prevent it from backsliding. Our guides drove the toes of their boots into the scree and secured their uphill foot this way. What worked better for us is a variation on going uphill with skis on, a skiing technique called the herringbone. On skis, one points the tips of the skis outwards and digs the inside edge of the advancing ski into the surface; after crossing over a rise, the pattern remaining in the snow indeed looks like a herringbone. Got the picture? So on the way up to Gilman's Point, point your toes out, like you're doing a Charlie Chaplin duck waddle, and dig the inside edge of your boot firmly into the scree. This should minimize backsliding. Grace doesn't count here.

Another technique that will help is to make proper use of your walking sticks. As you step forward with one foot, advance the contralateral (the other side) walking stick and dig it into the scree rather firmly. To some extent, you will be pulling yourself up. This is not as easy as it sounds. The confounding factor is related to oxygen deprivation. Your ability to concentrate on technique will be challenged. Be ready for some mental confusion and loss of coordination.

What would be optimal is to train climbing a pile of gravel. Ideally, find a gravel pile about 4,000 feet high and practice climbing up it. A shorter pile will do, but practicing what works best for you to get up scree will be very helpful.

As you start out from Kibo Hut in the middle of the night, it may not seem so cold. Some people who started out when we did thought it was too warm to take gloves; they had to turn back later. It gets colder and colder, more and more windy, as you ascend these last 4,000 feet. It's better to have too much clothing, and stuff it in your daypack later, than to not have enough.

You may recall that we named this part of the path The Snake. We calculated that it's a 27 percent slope. Try that out on your treadmill. It probably won't adjust that high! It's *really* steep. There is a straight line through The Snake, but this is used for descending, not ascending. You will be switching back and forth, forth and back, for what will seem like an eternity. So the nickname for this part of the path relates to its serpentine pattern. There is a respite about halfway up called Hans Mayer Cave. You will stop here for something to drink (tea) and maybe a snack.

It cannot be overemphasized that during this time it is imperative that you keep yourself hydrated. What we think works best is a carbohydrate-enriched drink that will help keep your energy level up. Your body will need energy and water. Also, water bottles tend to freeze up. An insulator for your water bottle will help. Keep your bottle under your parka and sip from it frequently.

Above The Snake is a stretch we called The Boulders. Not much description is needed here, but the technique is clambering from one big rock to another. You're wearing mittens or gloves anyway, because it's so cold, but you welcome the protection for your hands here. Compared to The Snake, you won't spend much time in The Boulders.

We advised you to do this at or soon after the full moon. This helps. If you are there at any other time of the lunar phase, a light source will be required. What works best is a headlamp, freeing your hands for your walking sticks, which you will find are being relied upon more and more.

It will be light by the time you get to Gilman's Point. The sunrise over Mawenzi, behind you, is spectacular! From here you can see Uhuru Peak. Our goal all along was to get to Uhuru, and it looked really far away! Except for the thin air, this part is pretty easy. But the thin air presents a serious challenge. One technique that is supposed to help is called "pressure breathing." As you exhale, purse your lips to create a backpressure. Your lungs "see" the air at this higher pressure as if you're at a lower altitude and can function more normally.

We hope that you have enough stamina at this point to trudge over from Gilman's Point to Uhuru Peak. You will know it when you get there. It's well marked. Congratulations! You're at the highest point on the African continent!

Mental techniques

It's easy to become discouraged. You will need something to keep your mind occupied. Hearing yourself pant for hours and hours does get repetitious. Neville Shulman has some useful suggestions for Zen techniques (see References: *Zen in the Art of Climbing Mountains*). We each had our little tricks. Susan memorized some of her favorite poetry to recite to herself, even reciting out loud a particular favorite by Robert Service when we got to the top. The poem is *The Rolling Stone*. Here is one verse:

> To scorn all strife, and to view all life,
> With the curious eyes of a child.
> From the plangent sea to the prairies,
> From the slum to the heart of the Wild.
> From the red-rimmed star to the speck of sand,
> From the vast to the greatly small;
> For I know that the whole for the good is planned,
> And I want to see it all.

I like to work at learning foreign languages so I counted to ten in as many languages as I could. These are listed in appendix C. You would be well advised to be prepared to occupy your mind. And enjoy the spectacular scenery while you're there!

In the free time we had at Mandara Hut and Horombo Hut, we mostly played cards and wrote in our diaries. This activity matched our limited attention spans. We each had a paperback book to read, but read very little. There is very little privacy, lots of hustle and bustle, and more than a little anxiety. Plus you're bone tired. But there is some down time, so be prepared to occupy it.

Photography

We could not imagine making this climb without a means of recording it photographically. On the other hand, this is a highly individual preference and we did see people on Mount Kilimanjaro without cameras.

Photography is a serious hobby of ours, so there was no debate on this issue in our minds. If you feel otherwise, skip to the next section. We brought five cameras with us, including a Nikon N90s with 20 mm and 35-80 mm AFD lenses. They worked great. If you're planning a safari in conjunction with your climb, you will also need longer lenses.

We also took an old Nikon F2 with a 200 mm macro lens and got some great shots of the flora, including a variety of impatiens (Impatiens kilimanjari) found only on Mount Kilimanjaro. We also have an old Realist stereo camera. These are hard to come by, but we got some fabulous stereo shots that put us back on top of Mount Kilimanjaro. If you are into stereo photography, you know that it's difficult to have stereo slides processed and mounted. The only place we know of for stereo processing is Rocky Mountain Film Lab, 560 Geneva St., Aurora, CO 80010. We also took a waterproof disposable camera as a back-up, but we didn't use it. We also had a disposable panoramic camera, but we were seriously disappointed in the results.

Choice of film is another highly individual decision. You will not need fast film (high ISO, what used to be called ASA) on Mount Kilimanjaro during the day (and why would you want to take a picture at night?). It's above the clouds and the light is strong, even harsh. What worked very well is Fuji Velvia film. It's slow (ISO 50) and very fine grained to give exceedingly sharp pictures. We also used Fuji Provia (ISO 100), but the Velvia was better. Because we were going on safari after the climb, we also took Professional Kodachrome (200 ISO) film, but you don't need this speed with short lenses on the mountain. Fine-grained film is best.

10 — Let's safari!

This is not a book about going on safari. This is a book about climbing Mount Kilimanjaro. *But,* since you're going to be over there, you might consider taking advantage of the rich zoological heritage of the region. We did, and had a fabulous time.

We made arrangements with Seamus Brice-Bennett directly through the Marangu Hotel. The morning after we got back off of Mount Kilimanjaro and got thoroughly cleaned up (this was a treat!), we were picked up by a driver/guide and a cook in an old Land Rover. They took us to Tarangire National Park, Lake Manyara National Park, the Serengeti National Park, and our favorite spot, Ngorongoro Crater. We ended up at Ngorongoro Sopa Lodge, a fancy place, particularly compared to our other accommodations in campgrounds. Then our driver

Bull elephant at close range. Our driver threw the vehicle into reverse right after this picture was taken.

*Lioness at
Ngorongoro Crater*

dropped us off at JRO (a full day's drive from Ngorongoro) and we went home. The fee for the safari was US$200 per day for the two of us plus US$20 per day each for park entrance fees and $20 per night for camping in the parks. (As we said before, small bills come in handy here. Change is given in Tanzanian shillings.) Reasonable, but this was not luxurious: actually, in some instances, it was less luxurious than on the mountain, if you can believe that. But the animals were incredible! If you have only a short time, go to Ngorongoro Crater. It's all there!

For more information on safaris, there are several good books out there. The one that was recommended to us was *East Africa Travel Survival Kit* from Lonely Planet (see References). We were told that the information in this book was accurate and reliable, and indeed it was.

"Giraffic Park" as we entered the Serengeti plains

11 — We'll never be the same

Was this experience what we thought it would be? No, not even close. It was so much more challenging and exhilarating than we ever, ever imagined. We are not talented enough to put into words what climbing Mount Kilimanjaro meant to us. It was rough; we got filthy dirty; it cost us a lot of money. We got into great physical shape. We saw things we've never seen before, hadn't even imagined before. We made it to the top.

We sincerely hope that this experience will mean as much to you as it did to us. We're planning to go back and climb the "Hard Way." Maybe we'll see you at Uhuru Peak!

Susan contemplating the task ahead as she looks out over the dramatic vista of The Saddle at Kibo Peak

Appendix A — Fitness training programme by Neville Shulman

The following four-week training programme is recommended by Neville Shulman and certainly will produce substantial benefits.

Week 1

Day 1: Two miles steady jogging

Day 2: Two/three miles steady jogging

Day 3: Three miles steady jogging plus press-up and sit-ups

Day 4: Half-hour swim or cycle or three miles jogging

Day 5: Three-mile run with exercises en route

Day 6: Hard three miles, alternating sprinting and jogging

Day 7: Quiet Day

Week 2

Day 1: Fast two miles jogging

Day 2: Four miles jogging

Day 3: One hour's walk carrying a 25-pound pack and boots

Day 4: Hour-long swim or cycle or four miles jogging with exercises en route

Day 5: Hard three miles jogging, varying the pace

Day 6: One/two hours walk carrying heavy pack and boots

Day 7: Quiet Day

Week 3

Day 1: Five miles slow jogging

Day 2: Two miles jogging with exercises en route

Day 3: Hour-long swim or cycle or four miles fast run

Day 4: Five miles slow jogging

Day 5: One/two hours walk carrying a 35-pound pack and boots

Day 6: Four miles hard running

Day 7: Quiet Day

Week 4

Day 1: One/two hours walk carrying a forty-pound pack and boots

Day 2: Five miles running, varying the pace and exercises en route

Day 3: One hour swim or cycle or four miles jogging

Day 4: Five miles slow jogging

Day 5: Six to eight miles jogging

Day 6: A full day's walk carrying a forty-pound pack and boots

Day 7: Quiet Day

In addition to your general training, use the following series of leg and knee exercises to strengthen the ligaments around the knees, the calves, and the ankles, all those areas that will endure a great deal of use and punishment on the mountain.

1. Initially step up and step down in rapid succession using a low bench or a step.

2. Hop at speed across a room, forwards and then backwards, alternating to each foot.

3. Using ankle weights, raise each foot in turn, first from a lying position, then from a sitting position, finally from a standing position.

4. If your legs become really strong enough, as this is on the most difficult and strenuous exercises, hop up a flight of stairs on one leg, walk down and then repeat on the other leg. (Those who can and must could try two stairs at a time.)

Each of the above exercises to be carried out within a set time for up to twenty times each day.

As published in his book *On Top of Africa, The Climbing of Kilimanjaro and Mt. Kenya.* Reproduced with permission.

Appendix B — A complete list of items to take

Documents

Tickets: airline, train passes for Switzerland

Passports: expiration date checked

Visas for Tanzania

Vaccination records: these were checked upon arrival at JRO

Traveler's checks

Cash, including small bills

Credit cards: expiration date extended

Reservation confirmations for hotels in Amsterdam, Switzerland, and Marangu Hotel

Address list: to send post cards, etc.

Health insurance card

Medical supplies

Personal prescription medications

Lariam (antimalarial; requires prescription)

Diamox® (to prevent altitude sickness; requires prescription)

Cipro (powerful antibiotic, just in case; requires prescription)

Loperamide hydrochloride (antidiarrheal; brand names include Imodium A-D, Maalox Antidiarrheal, Pepto Diarrhea Control)

Bismuth subsalicylate tablets (Pepto-Bismol or generic equivalent; tablets are more convenient than the liquid)

Analgesics (pain killers; pick your favorite, Tylenol, Ibuprofen, etc.; oral morphine, if you can get a prescription, in the event of a serious injury)

Sleeping pills (to sleep on the plane, help deal with jet lag)

Cortisone ointment (for rashes, insect bites, etc.)

Antifungal cream (for athlete's foot or other fungal infections)

Antibacterial ointment (for cuts, etc.)

Sterile alcohol wipes

Cotton balls

Lamb's wool (to put between your toes)

Band-Aids, ACE wraps, and/or Steri-Strips (or comparable wound dressing supplies)

New-Skin Liquid Bandage (comes in a small bottle, or even better, 1-ml. packets for single use; great stuff for blisters, etc.)

Antihistamines and/or decongestants

Syringes and needles (in case you need an injection of snake antivenom, etc.; do not expect too much in the way of local medical supplies)

Photography equipment

Nikon N90s body

20 mm AFD lens with UV filter

35-80 zoom AFD lens with UV filter

Nikon F2 body with 200 mm macro lens

Velvia, 6 rolls (ISO 50 film that worked particularly well)

Provia, 6 rolls (ISO 100 film that worked almost as well)

Kodachrome film, 20 rolls (ISO 200 professional film for safari, not for mountain)

Susan using a macro lens to photograph some of the small flowers on Mount Kilimanjaro

Disposable waterproof camera (a backup; didn't use)

Disposable panoramic camera (a disappointment)

Realist stereo camera

Binoculars (didn't use them on the mountain)

Warm weather clothes

Nylon shorts

Long nylon safari pants, with zip-off legs

Long sleeve T-shirts, 2 pair

Denim shirt

Walking or running shoes (for lower path)

Socks, 2 pair

Underwear, 4 pair

Wide-brim hat

Baseball cap

Sunglasses, with 100 percent UV protection

Cotton gloves or weight-lifting gloves (to use with walking sticks)

Bandannas (several)

Cold weather clothes

LIFA™ long underwear, top and bottom

Furnace shirt

Furnace pants

Snow pants

Sweatshirt (with hood) or polar fleece pullover (with hood)

Parka and/or windbreaker; Columbia and Stearns make good products

Wool hat

Balaclava, silk

Boots, well broken in

Sock liners, 3 pair

Socks, heavy, 3 pair

Rain jacket

Glove liners

Mittens

Ski goggles

Gear

Sleeping bags with sacks (rated to 0°F)

Mini pillow cases (stuff clothes into them and they're pillows)

Mats, self-inflating, 3/4 length

Water bottles, insulated, 2-liter (quart) bottles per person

Headlamp

Dive lights

Backpack

Daypack

Walking sticks

Stuff sacks, various sizes and colors (to keep stuff organized)

Extra batteries

Personal stuff (toiletries)

100 percent DEET (insect repellent)

Sunscreen (SPF 50 and SPF 30; absolutely essential)

Chapstick, with sunscreen

Toothbrush, toothpaste

Eyedrops

Ricola cough drops (lots of them; important to suck on at altitude where the air is very dry, also to share with guides)

Soap, washcloth, and small towel (bandannas work, but towel would be better; linen or chamois-like is much better than terrycloth)

Shampoo (to use before and after the climb, not during)

Tissues (Kleenex)

Towelletes

Matches

Sewing kit (for repairs, plus a needle for lancing blisters)

Toilet paper (don't count on there being any available)

Depend incontinence products (if anticipated)

Feminine hygiene products (women only)

Zip-lock bags (to keep this stuff organized, and visible; later used for disposing of garbage)

More personal stuff (This list must be personalized)

Maps (topographical map of Mount Kilimanjaro and road map of Tanzania)

Guide books

Climbing Mount Kilimanjaro (you're holding it right now!)

Tape player (Walkman) with cassettes (makes a treasured gift)

Journal or diary, with pencils (ink tends to smudge if it gets wet.)

Paperback books

Playing cards

Food

Powders to flavor water (Gatorade, lemon crystals, etc.)

Powders with carbohydrate supplements (for energy)

Iodine purification tablets (to treat drinking water; the flavored powders are to mask the iodine taste)

Energy bars (Power Bars, granola, etc.)

Instant coffee (enough to share)

Instant cocoa

Instant breakfast and/or powdered (skim) milk

Trail mix (make your own)

Gifts (to give to guides, porters, etc.)

T-shirts from home

Post cards of your home town

Baseball caps

Cassette tapes

Lighters

Clicky (ball-point) pens

Stickers (for children)

(We are personally opposed to tobacco products, but they are highly valued gifts)

Appendix C — Mind games
or
Counting to 10 in several different languages
or
How to keep your mind occupied

ARABIC

One	Waahid
Two	Ihnayn
Three	Thalaatha
Four	Arbaa
Five	Khamsa
Six	Sitta
Seven	Sabaa
Eight	Thamaanya
Nine	Tisa
Ten	Ashra

DUTCH

One	Een
Two	Twee
Three	Drie
Four	Vier
Five	Vijf
Six	Zes
Seven	Zeven
Eight	Acht
Nine	Negen
Ten	Tien

GERMAN

One	Eins
Two	Zwei
Three	Drei
Four	Vier
Five	Funf
Six	Sechs
Seven	Sieben
Eight	Acht
Nine	Neun
Ten	Zehn

CHINESE (Mandarin)

One	Yi
Two	Ér
Three	San
Four	Sz
Five	Wu
Six	Lyòu
Seven	Chi
Eight	Ba
Nine	Jyou
Ten	Shr

FRENCH

One	Un
Two	Deux
Three	Trois
Four	Quatre
Five	Cinq
Six	Six
Seven	Sept
Eight	Huit
Nine	Neuf
Ten	Dix

GREEK

One	Ehna
Two	Dío
Three	Tría
Four	Tésera
Five	Pénte
Six	Éxí
Seven	Eptá
Eight	Ohktó
Nine	Enéa
Ten	Déka

This information was extracted, with permission, from booklets provided by T² Travel Tapes™. This company puts out booklets and cassette tapes with essential phrases for the traveler. They don't have a tape for Africa yet, but they have, or will soon have, tapes for Western Europe, Eastern Europe, the Far East, and Southeast Asia. We have tried out the tapes and they are very handy.

HUNGARIAN

One	Egy
Two	Kettö
Three	Hàrom
Four	Négy
Five	Öt
Six	Hat
Seven	Hét
Eight	Nyolc
Nine	Kilenc
Ten	Tìz

POLISH

One	Jeden
Two	Dwa
Three	Trzy
Four	Cztery
Five	Piec
Six	Szesc
Seven	Siedem
Eight	Osiem
Nine	Dziewiec
Ten	Dziesiec

SPANISH

One	Uno
Two	Dos
Three	Tres
Four	Cuatro
Five	Cinco
Six	Seis
Seven	Siete
Eight	Ocho
Nine	Nueve
Ten	Diez

ITALIAN

One	Uno
Two	Due
Three	Tre
Four	Quattro
Five	Cinque
Six	Sei
Seven	Sette
Eight	Otto
Nine	Nove
Ten	Dieci

PORTUGUESE

One	Um
Two	Dois
Three	Três
Four	Quatro
Five	Cinco
Six	Seis
Seven	Sete
Eight	Oito
Nine	Nove
Ten	Dez

SWEDISH

One	En
Two	Två
Three	Tre
Four	Fyra
Five	Fem
Six	Sex
Seven	Sju
Eight	Åtta
Nine	Nio
Ten	Tio

JAPANESE

One	Ichi
Two	Ni
Three	San
Four	Yon
Five	Go
Six	Roku
Seven	Shichi
Eight	Hachi
Nine	Kyu
Ten	Jyu

RUSSIAN

One	Odyn
Two	Dwa
Three	Tree
Four	Cheteerye
Five	Pyat
Six	Shest
Seven	Sem
Eight	Vosem
Nine	Devyat
Ten	Desyat

THAI

One	Nung
Two	Song
Three	Sarm
Four	Seeh
Five	Ha
Six	Hoak
Seven	Jed
Eight	Paat
Nine	Gow
Ten	Sib

References and guidebooks

Guide to Mount Kenya and Kilimanjaro, Edited by Iain Allan, Mountain Club of Kenya, © 1990 Mountain Club of Kenya
ISBN #9966-9856-0-3
Library of Congress Catalog No. 90-980316
Distributed by:
> The Mountain Club of Kenya
> P.O. Box 45741
> Nairobi, Kenya

Available from:
> Adventurous Traveler Bookstore
> P.O. Box 1468
> Williston, Vermont 05495
> Phone: (800) 282-3963
> FAX: (800) 677-1821
> Internet: http://www.AdventurousTraveler.com
> email: books@atbook.com
> (Topographic maps of Mount Kilimanjaro are also available from this store.)

Zen in the Art of Climbing Mountains, by Neville Shulman, © 1992 Neville Shulman
ISBN #0-8048-1775-8
Published by:
> Charles E. Tuttle Company, Inc.
> 153 Milk Street
> Boston, Massachusetts 02109

High Altitude Illness and Wellness, The History and Prevention of a Killer, by Charles Houston, M.D., © 1993 Charles S. Houston
ISBN #0-934802-72-6
Published by:
> ICS Books, Inc.
> P.O. Box 10767
> 1370 E. 86th Place, Merrillville, IN 46410
> Phone: (800) 541-7323
> FAX: (800) 336-8334
> Internet: http://www.onlinesports.com

"Nutrition for Winter Sports" (pp. 22-33), and "Nutrition for High Altitudes and Mountain Sports" (pp. 383-392), by Julie Ann Lickteig, in *Winter Sports Medicine*, M.J. Casey, C. Foster, & E.G. Hixson, editors, 1990.
ISBN 0-8036-1638-X
Published by:
> F.A. Davis Company
> 1915 Arch Street
> Philadelphia, PA 19103
> Phone: (800) 523-4049
> (215) 568-2270 from Pennsylvania, Hawaii, or Alaska

Seven Summits, by Dick Bass & Frank Wells with Rick Ridgeway, © 1986 Frank Wells and Dick Bass
ISBN # 0-446-38516-6
Published by:
> Warner Books, Inc.
> 1271 Avenue of the Americas
> New York, N.Y. 10020

Swahili Phrasebook, by Robert Leonard, © 1987 Lonely Planet
ISBN # 0-86442-025-0
Published by:
> Lonely Planet Publications
> P.O. Box 2001A
> Berkeley, CA 94702 USA

Phrasebook and cassette available from:
> Adventurous Traveler Bookstore (see above)

East Africa Travel Survival Kit, by Geoff Crowther and Hugh Finlay, © 1994 Lonely Planet
ISBN #0-86442-209-1
Published by:
> Lonely Planet Publications
> P.O. Box 2001A
> Berkeley, CA 94702 USA

Index

A solitary giraffe at Lake Manyara

Notes

Notes